Dolls' House Furniture

Easy-to-make projects in 1/12 scale

Freida Gray

GUILD OF
MASTER CRAFTSMAN
PUBLICATIONS

First published 2002 by
Guild of Master Craftsman Publications Ltd
166 High Street Lewes
East Sussex BN7 1XU

Reprinted 2003, 2005

ISBN 1 86108 258 4

A catalogue record for this book is available from the British Library.

Editor: David Arscott
Book and cover design: Grant Bradford and Sam Reeves

Colour origination by Viscan Graphics (Singapore)

Printed and bound in Singapore by Kyodo Printing Co. Ltd.

Dolls' House
Furniture

Contents

How information is presented

Same size drawings

Throughout this book the component drawings are printed the same size as they should be cut, so that they can be used in various ways.

1 As cutting templates if you don't like a lot of measuring. Some also serve as templates for card or fabric covering. Photocopies are useful for this. Carefully transfer the lines to the material using dressmakers carbon paper and a fine pointed pencil, and for straight lines use a ruler.

2 Trying to covert between imperial and metric measurements using a conversion table is not always satisfactory, as this gives only an approximation. Measuring the component drawings should give much more accurate results.

3 Photocopies can be used to give drawings for other scales, which can then be measured in either metric or imperial.
See 'Other Sizes', facing page.

Colour codes

Throughout all the component drawings, the thickness of the material is indicated by the same colour code. Therefore everywhere the component is cut from say ⅛in thick wood, the component drawing will be coloured green; for ³⁄₃₂in thick the component will be coloured pink, and so on. The complete colour code is shown below.

Colour codes and symbols

The thickness of wood to be used for each component is indicated by the colour used on the drawing. The original wood was in imperial sizes as listed.

�	¹⁄₆₄in		³⁄₁₆in
	¹⁄₃₂in		¼in
	¹⁄₁₆in		⅜in
	³⁄₃₂in		½in
	⅛in		¾in

Other components are coloured as shown below

	Turned items		Mirror material or clear plastic
	Mouldings		Background for shaping

Grain direction is indicated by arrows ↕ ↔

The number of components needed is shown in brackets e.g. (4)

Introduction

Have you ever wanted to have a go at making your own dolls' house furniture but thought it was too tricky to tackle? Well, it isn't necessarily as complicated or difficult as it may at first appear, so don't just sit there: have a go at it, and you might surprise yourself.

By carefully choosing the items of furniture and the style or period, there is a lot that can be done successfully with even the minimum of tools and equipment, and with no previous knowledge or experience of making models or miniatures. Although for some items it is useful, or even necessary, to have a wide range of equipment and power tools, these are not always essential in order to produce some very satisfactory and pleasing results. Much of the success in making miniatures of any kind depends just as much, if not more, on ingenuity and patience as on having lots of expensive equipment. A certain degree of manual dexterity is obviously essential, but without these three – manual dexterity, ingenuity, and patience – a whole workshop full of equipment will not enable you to produce successful miniatures.

As far as materials are concerned, these are easily obtained nowadays in the small sizes needed for miniature furniture making, and they are not exorbitantly expensive in the quantities you will need.

This book takes you from making simple furniture, with the minimum of basic tools and equipment, to creating more ambitious projects requiring a greater range of equipment and the skill to use it.

1:12 Scale

For most of us it is sufficient to be able to make satisfactory looking pieces of furniture to grace a 1:12 scale dolls' house, and what matters to us is the look of the thing. Actually trying to scale down all the measurements from a 'real' piece of furniture is, of course, quite simple mathematically – just measure and divide by 12. This is generally not practicable, however, any more than it is feasible in many cases to follow the original methods of construction.

Deciding what is right for a 1:12 scale miniature can be simplified. By getting a few basic proportions correct, you can gauge the proportions for the rest of the piece. If you have a 3in diameter table (the true scale size for a 3ft table), and you find that four cups and saucers fill it, then there is clearly something wrong with the size of the cups and saucers.

Conversely, put four correctly scaled dinner plates (about ¾in to ⅞in diameter) on what is supposed to be a scale-size dining table. If you have no room for any cutlery or other tableware, then there must be something wrong with the size of the table. With just a few correct items, it as simple as that to see where the scale size of something else is right or wrong.

Other sizes

If you wish to make furniture in either of the other popular scales, the full size 1:12 drawings can be reduced. A photocopier or computer scanner makes this reduction easy. For 1:16 scale you need 75% of the 1:12 scale size, and for 1:24 scale you want just 50 per cent. This gives ¾in to the foot and ½in to the foot respectively. While the overall sizes will be correct, the thickness of material will also be reduced proportionately. This may mean that the exact scale size is not available or would be far too thin to be practicable. With the plan views and assembly views on the drawings, it should not present too much difficulty to substitute suitable thicknesses of material and adjust the sizes of adjacent bits accordingly.

Desks made in the popular scales of 1:12, 1:16 and 1:24.

SAFETY

Before you start working on any of the projects, please do read the notes that follow. Read them again if you start to use the powertools described on page 97. Some of the things listed here may seem almost too obvious to mention, but following a few simple rules can save no end of heartache. Please never forget safety.

Basic Safety Rules

- Any tool can be a potential danger if not stored and handled properly, and all materials are potentially dangerous if misused or if they get into the wrong hands. Since many of the materials used in this hobby are attractive to look at, make sure that tools are kept out of the reach of children at all times.

- Both cleanliness and tidiness are essential for safety. Don't try to work with tools in a cluttered area: you are much more likely to cut something wrongly or, worse still, cut yourself.

- After working, always wash your hands thoroughly before eating or putting your fingers in your mouth: you don't know what may be on them from some of the materials used, or what damage this could do.

- Never smoke while working. There is always a fire risk, and material can be transferred from your fingers to a cigarette and thence to your mouth.

- Work in a good light, not ordinary room light. It is much easier to cut yourself if you can't see what you are doing properly.

- Always follower manufacturers' and suppliers' instructions for the use and storage of materials and equipment

- Make sure that all electrical equipment is wired correctly, has the correct value fuse fitted, and that the supply cable is not damaged in any way. If in doubt, consult a qualified electrician.

- Protect your lungs from sanding dust and paint spray by wearing a face mask.

- Keep magnifiers covered and out of the direct rays of the sun in case you start a fire.

Last words before you begin

Please keep safety in mind at all times. Don't rush. Work with care, thoroughness and patience: this is not only the safest practice, but it leads to the most satisfactory end result.

Tools and Equipment

ESSENTIALS

For each item of furniture I have noted the minimum hand tools and equipment. The few absolutely essential items are a craft set, a drill and drill bits, a metal ruler, a small square and some small files.

There are other items such as glue, stain, paint, abrasive paper, emery boards, scissors etc., many of which you may already have somewhere. Of course, if you have other equipment, or would like to improve your tool kit then there is a wide choice of tools which will make the job easier or quicker, or which will give a more professional look to your furniture. More detailed information is given below, and information on miniature power tools can be found on page 98.

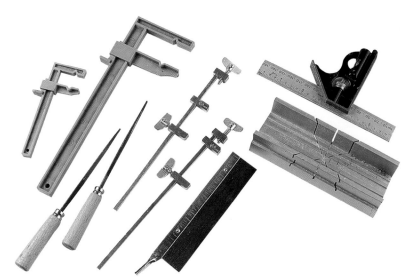

A selection of useful handtools: plastic clamps, files, bar clamps, razor saw blade, mitre box, combination square.

Craft set

These come in a variety of guises. The one I used in making the furniture described contained a number of craft knife handles and a wide selection of inter-changeable blades (including chisel blades and razor saw blades), sanding blocks and a mitre box. (Without a mitre box it is very difficult to get a good, square cut and it will also enable you to make accurate cuts at 45°.)

Hand fretsaw

If you don't have any power tools, this is a very useful tool for cutting intricate shapes and curves. Hand fretsaws may take a while to get used to, however. They can be bought quite cheaply in a complete set, which includes instructions for their use.

Files and abrasives

A set of needle files can now be bought reasonably cheaply, and should be adequate. As for abrasive papers, there is a vast array of different kinds and grit sizes. The ones that I use are an open coat abrasive of 240 grit, and silicone carbide (wet and dry) in various grades from 400 to 1200 grit. Both are widely available in model shops, DIY stores, etc. Remember that the bigger the number of the grit size, the finer the abrasive paper.

Drill

You will need a small hand drill, or even a pin chuck, together with a few small drill bits. These can usually be bought at model shops.

Ruler

Metal rules are the most useful, as they are more accurate than the plastic variety and can also serve as a straightedge cutting guide for use with a craft knife.

Square

A small engineer's square is ideal, but it is possible to manage with a plastic setsquare, such as those which come in school drawing sets.

Clamps

Miniature clamps are available from model shops, and are not very expensive. For some items miniature sash cramps are an advantage because of their longer reach. These are also usually available from model shops, and both can be bought by mail-order.

Pencil

You will also need a pencil, which should be kept well sharpened. I prefer to use a pencil of 'F' grade rather than the more usual 'HB', because the lines come out much finer.

Materials

ESSENTIALS

As for materials, we again begin by keeping things simple,
the following being all you need:

- Balsa wood • Basswood • Model plywood • Fabric and felt
- Synthetic wadding • Card or plastic sheet • Adhesive • Paint or other wood finish

If you would like to use different types of wood, then the choice is yours.
More information about some of the materials follows for those who are interested in having more detail.

Wood

If you have the facilities, by far the cheapest way of getting the sections of wood that you want is to cut them yourself from much larger timber. Few of us can do this, however. Luckily, there are many sections, in various types of wood, which can now be bought ready-cut to size.

The woods most commonly available are obeche, ramin, basswood (lime), walnut, mahogany and oak. Some companies also have more exotic woods such as American cherry. Pine and balsa are also very easily obtained, but I do not recommend them for general purpose use. Pine is very resinous, and this tends to 'gum up' tools and equipment. Balsa is useful as a basis for quickly made upholstered furniture where the wood is completely covered.

To start with, I would suggest either basswood (lime), or obeche. Both are fairly easy to cut, and they will give you two completely different kinds of grain. Lime has a very close, even grain, which makes it easier to get a smooth finish to paintwork, while Obeche has a somewhat more open grain with clear definition, and this can be attractive for a polished furniture look.

Mouldings and turned wooden items

Pre-machined wooden mouldings of all kinds, suitable for 1:12 scale and, to a lesser extent, 1:24 scale, are available from a number of suppliers. Many dolls' house shops stock a selection of these. They are invaluable in achieving some of the nicer finishing touches. It is possible to make them yourself, or to cut them directly onto the components used in making a piece of furniture, but this is not practicable without accurate, high-speed power equipment. I would therefore advise sticking to the professionally produced mouldings.

Other very useful wooden parts which can be bought are turned items such as staircase newel posts and balusters – although in the context of this book you will not be using them for the purpose for which they were intended. Some firms also sell ready-turned table legs, knobs, etc., which can make your project much more simple to produce, and give a really superb finish to a piece of furniture.

Furniture fittings

There is a good range of brass or brassed (brass-coated) fittings available for miniature furniture, such as tiny hinges, knobs, draw-pulls, etc. These can usually be found in model shops or dolls' house shops, and can give your furniture that final touch of realism.

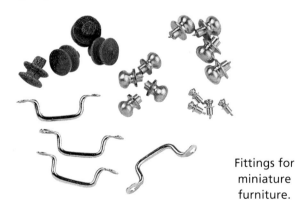

Fittings for miniature furniture.

Fabrics

For upholstery on miniature furniture it is not usually advisable to try to use the real thing. It is often far too clumsy to be effective. There are various ways of getting round this, and I would suggest collecting small pieces of fine fabric, either plain or with a very tiny pattern. Many kinds of miniature braids and trimmings are available from specialist suppliers. However, many trimmings, ribbons and lace, available from sewing shops, can be used or modified. Look out for wide, patterned ribbons that could be used for such things as chair seats.

Fabrics suitable for miniature upholstered furniture.

The same shops will sell synthetic wadding, in various thicknesses, which is good for padding miniature upholstery. The different types of Vilene (a dressmaker's stiffener) are also very useful: because this material is non-woven, it doesn't fray.

Adhesive

For sticking wood together, I have found that there is nothing better than a PVA glue of some kind. They dry clear, and any excess glue can easily be removed, before it dries, with a damp cloth. Once set properly, however, the joint is often stronger than the wood surrounding it. Whichever brand you use, a fast-setting type is the one I have found best for small items.

A clear, general purpose glue, such as UHU or Bostick clear, can be useful for fixing some upholstery and trimmings, but a PVA glue will often also serve this purpose better. For fabric a thick PVA glue called decorator glue or tacky glue that doesn't mark the fabric is particularly useful.

Super-glues of all kinds are now readily available, and are very useful for sticking together dissimilar materials such as metal and wood. They need to be handled very carefully, as they bond almost immediately (with fingers, too). The one I use mostly is Zap-a-Gap, which, as its name implies, has a degree of gap-filling capability. In any case, I would recommend that you follow the manufacturers' instructions very carefully, and buy a bottle of a proprietary 'unstick' product, just in case you get it wrong.

Useful adhesives, paints and sanding sealers.

WOOD FINISHES

Sanding sealers

Although sanding sealers are not strictly wood finishes, they are extremely useful – particularly the shellac-based ones. Used to seal the wood before the final finish, they can be sanded to give a lovely surface for painting on to, and the paint doesn't just disappear into the wood.

Paints

Many model paints are available which are very good for finishing miniature furniture. Avoid very glossy ones for most projects, however, as they don't always look right in small-scale work. A silk or satin finish is often better. Spray paints are also useful, but must be used with great care. I use car spray paints. About the only colour I can't get (not surprising for car sprays) is pale pink.

Varnishes

Spray varnish or lacquer is also very good for giving stained furniture a final finish. Again, though, avoid using a high gloss one for most things. A satin finish looks better, except, perhaps, for a dining table top, when a gloss finish might be wanted.

Stains

Wood stains are available from the paint department of many stores. There are many makes and types, so I suggest that a little experimentation will soon tell you which one you like best. I use mostly Colron, and have found it satisfactory where I only want to apply one coat.

There is also what are called 'fadeless wood dyes'. I have found these very good for special effects, such as where I want to give an 'aged' look and therefore want to apply more than one coat in very small areas.

Polishes

It's possible to use French polish on miniature furniture, and there are even types available especially for miniaturists. It is, however, somewhat fiddly and messy, and you may find that a decent even finish is difficult to achieve, except on large flat areas such as table tops, for which it is excellent.

Wax

Some items look best if they are simply given a good waxed finish, and there are many available for the woodworker. The ones I find most useful are those that come in a touch-up size, which is ideal for miniature furniture.

Construction
Basics

Before getting too involved in individual pieces of furniture, let's spare a moment to go through some of the technical bits about making furniture of the miniature kind, which may not be the same as its full-size cousin. Although you may be using card, metal, plastic or some other material, most furniture is wooden, and this is the aspect on which I have concentrated.

Joining wood

There are many different kinds of joints used in real-size woodwork. With great care and skill most of these can be used in making miniatures, but they are generally far too complicated and not at all necessary for a realistic looking result. Very careful measuring and cutting will allow you to make furniture by simply butting the surfaces together with a suitable glue, such as PVA or Aliphatic glues, and holding or clamping them in place until the glue sets. For anyone who is keen to use more 'correct' joints I will give you a brief outline.

Butt joint

What is generally listed as being the simplest, is the butt joint, which is more or less self-explanatory: the two pieces to be joined are simply butted together and glued in place. This is not always as simple as it sounds, because unless the pieces are cut extremely accurately you will not get a very strong joint – particularly where you are joining the end of one piece to the side of another.

Other joints

There are two types of joint which, somewhat modified, I use quite a lot in order to get a stronger joint. The full-size versions are called 'mortice and tenon' and (the more modern) 'biscuit' joints. Another option I use is to add either wooden or brass dowels, turning them into a sort of dowel joint.

Mortice and tenon

The real-size mortice and tenon joint can be made using a tenon saw and wood chisel, or by sophisticated machinery. In miniature work the mortice can be made by using a drill to remove most of the material, and a craft knife or file to square-up the corners. Tenons can be cut by first marking the 'shoulder line' with a craft knife, and then using a razor saw or craft knife to remove the rest of the material.

Biscuit joint

The full-size biscuit joint needs a special tool to cut semi-circular slots in the two pieces of wood to be joined, and a special 'biscuit' which fits these slots and is glued into them to hold the joint firmly together. I find that in situations where a biscuit joint or mortice and tenon joint might be used to advantage, a narrow strip of 1/64in thick model ply can be used in a similar way, glued into slits made with a craft knife. The ply gives an additional internal area for the glue and strengthens the joint. Ply is first glued into one slit, trimmed to length, and then glue is applied both to the strip and to the area of the joint before clamping the joint together.

Dowel joint

Sometimes joints can be strengthened by using dowels, another option employed in some places for full-sized articles. It is not often possible to use wooden dowels in miniatures because of the small sizes needed. If the pieces of wood are big enough, sections of wooden cocktail sticks can be used. For smaller sections of wood, brass rod or fine panel pins can be used with an appropriate adhesive. Note that you will need accurate placement of the holes for the dowels, and the ability to make holes of a suitable size. The joint is assembled and glued together in a similar way to the biscuit joint above.

Housing joints

Some form of housing joint is a great advantage to the rigidity and strength of furniture, even in miniatures – always provided, of course, that you have the necessary tools, equipment and know-how. However, most of the pieces included here can be made using only plain butt joints, which is adequate for many purposes, although they do rely entirely on the accuracy of the cutting and the strength of the glue.

Rabbet (rebate)

This is a recess or step, usually right-angled, which is cut along the edges of a piece of wood. It is most useful for holding the back of a cabinet, so that it gives a strong joint and is not seen from the side of the piece of furniture. You can cut rabbets by hand, but by far the best way is to use a router fitted with a straight bit.

Dado (common housing joint, groove)

Cut across the grain of the wood, this is really just a groove to accept the end of another piece of wood. The lip of the groove gives some support to the second piece, and the area for the glue is increased. It can also accommodate wood where the end is not completely flush and as square as one would like. It can be cut by hand, but a more uniform result will be achieved if a router is used with the correct size of bit for the piece you want to fit to it.

Note: Unless the drawings actually say so, there is no allowance made for the extra bits needed if you want to use some of the other joints, so do remember to add this on where necessary.

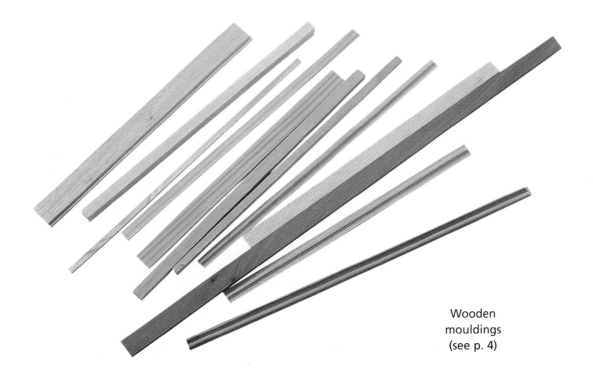

Wooden
mouldings
(see p. 4)

Easy Upholstered Furniture

For those of you who are not particularly happy with their woodworking skills I have chosen to start with a selection of items where you need nothing more technical than a craft knife and abrasive. It is all covered up by fabric and padding anyway, and this can hide a multitude of sins.

Those who are not sewing enthusiasts may be pleased to know that no sewing is involved in the methods I use for creating an upholstered look. Only in some of the optional home-made trimmings does a needle and thread come into it.

Simple upholstery

This is usually a matter of coming up with some material and/or method that gives a 'scale' look of the real thing. It is rarely possible to use either the same material or the same methods as in full size: it either doesn't look right, or doesn't work because of the size. Very often the most effective is also the easiest method, which helps.

Padded seating

To create a padded effect it is usually only necessary to place a thin layer of synthetic wadding or thin foam on top of the underlying structure, then cover it with fabric of some kind. I find that realistic results can be achieved by working on a balsa basis. This is very soft and easy to cut, sand and shape, giving a ready-shaped underlying form for the padding and covering. For rounded padding over the edges, cut the cellulose wadding larger and carry it over the edge.

Tip: If you do not have the correct thickness of balsa for the project, any combination of thicknesses glued together to the total thickness needed will serve just as well: 3 x ¼in. for ¾in base or ¼in plus ⅛in for ⅜in, and so on.

Fabric-covered card and padded-covered card (see facing page)

To achieve a neat finish with no frayed edges showing, it is often best to cover a piece of card with fabric and then stick this on to the piece of furniture in the appropriate place. I use the buff folders sold for office use, but any card of similar thickness will do. Many of your old greetings cards could be recycled for this purpose.

1   Cut the card to size, and a piece of fabric about ¼in larger all round.

2   Glue the fabric onto the card with an even overlap all round. Trim across the corners (see drawing). Where a degree of padding is needed, a layer of synthetic padding can be placed between the fabric and the card.

Tip: If you are using a distinctly patterned fabric, careful placement can make all the difference to the look of the finished article.

3   Snip any curved portions (see drawing).

4   Apply glue to the fabric and stick neatly to the back of the card. Where a snipped curve is met with, pull the fabric as close as possible to the curved shape and try to have as few layers of fabric as possible when gluing down.

Tip: A slightly softer feel can be given to the piece if you use iron-on Vilene instead of card in steps 1 and 2 above.

Note: This procedure comes in useful in many upholstered items, so to avoid ceaseless repetition I call this 'Fabric-covered card'.

In some cases a padded effect is also needed, so synthetic wadding or thin foam are interposed between the fabric and the card. This variation I call 'Padded-covered card'.

Buttoning and pleats

A buttoned, pleated or quilted effect can be gained quite easily by using a method based on padded-covered card. First stick the wadding to thin card with double-sided tape, add a piece of fabric somewhat larger all round than the card, and stitch through the lot, carrying the thread from one place to the next across the back of the card.

Trimmings

Narrow braid and trimmings can be bought from specialist suppliers. Some suggestions for home-made trimmings and braids can be found in the chapter Trimmings (page 151). They can be fixed in place with a little Tacky Glue (PVA) or Decorators' Glue (Thick PVA). It is also surprising how effective some knitting or embroidery yarns can be when simply used as they are.

Tip: To stiffen yarn or trim, run the yarn through a 50/50 mix of PVA and water; run the yarn through your fingers to remove any excess and even it out; then hang it up to dry.

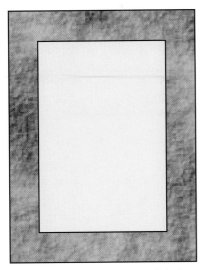

Cut card to suit, then cut fabric, allowing about ¼in to ⅜in all round for the turn-over.

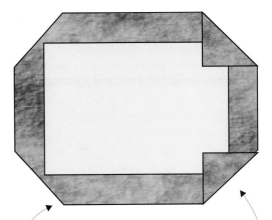

To help neaten the corners as the fabric is folded over the card either: (a) snip fabric away across the corner (not too close though), or (b) fold the corner of the fabric over first.

Snip from the outside edge almost to the card around curves, as often as necessary to achieve a neat turn-over, as flat as possible.

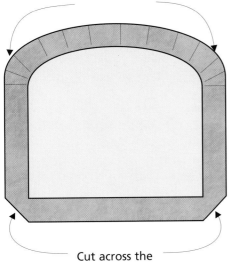

Cut across the corners to remove as much bulk of fabric as possible, to help keep a nice flat turn-over. Don't get too close to the card though.

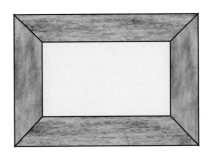

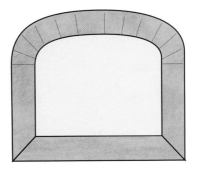

The final result should be as neat and flat as possible.

Divan

MATERIALS	TOOLS
Balsa ½in and ¾ in thick	Ruler and pencil
Fabric	Craft set
Synthetic wadding	Abrasive
or foam	Scissors
Glue	
Card	
Optional trim	

Making a pretty divan really couldn't be simpler. The basis is a block of balsa ¾in thick. This can be made up from a combination of layers of whatever thickness balsa you have to hand, so long as the finished result is the correct thickness. Naturally, the thicker the layers the better: you don't want to be sticking 12 layers of ⅟₁₆in thick.

This divan has been left plain, with no pleated valance, but is still an attractive piece.

METHOD

1 Cut the base shape from as many pieces of balsa as is needed to make up the required ¾in thickness. Glue them one on top of the other to form a block. Cut four foot pieces: these would be better cut from harder wood if you have any. They look best stained and varnished, but, as they will not show much, they could be painted.

2 Sand the corners of the base to shape, and sand the edges smooth.

3 A strip of fabric about 16in long and 1½in wide will be needed to cover the sides of the block.

4 Stick the strip of fabric around the block, applying the glue as you go, with the fabric overlapping evenly either side. Start in the centre of one long edge and work your way round, sticking the overlapping join at the end firmly to the start of the fabric strip.

5 Glue the overlap top and bottom to the surface of the block, in the same way as covering card (see p. 11), snipping corners where necessary.

6 The feet can now be stuck on close to each corner of what will become the bottom of the divan.

7 If you don't want the pleated valance effect, go straight to step 10.

For a pleated valance, cut a strip of fabric (or strips if you don't have one piece long enough) to fit around the divan base at least twice. Turn over and glue in place, a narrow hem along one long side (or sides if you have cut more than one strip).

Tip: Wundaweb or similar can make this job quicker and less messy. Cut strips about ¼in wide and use as per the manufacturers' instructions.

8 Pleat the strip evenly around the divan base, with the hem level with the bottom of the divan, gluing just the top ¼in of the pleats to the divan base. If you are using a number of strips, arrange it so that the joins come under the pleats.

Tip: Use pins to hold the pleats temporarily until satisfied everything is even and level. The pins should push easily into the balsa sufficiently to hold whilst you make adjustments, then glue as above.

9 Turn over the overlap and stick to the top of the base block as in step 5 above.

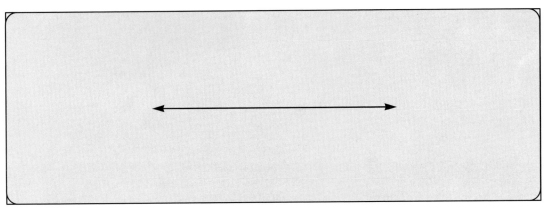

Top (1) - balsa ½in thick

Base (1) - balsa ¾in thick

Brown areas show the shape for both the base and top

Foot (4)

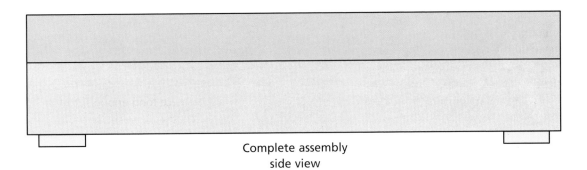

Complete assembly
side view

10 Now prepare the top block, made up of layers if needs be, in the same way as the base block, and cover the edges with fabric as in step 4 above, but with a strip of fabric only 1in wide.

11 Glue the top block on top of the base block.

12 Prepare a piece of padded covered card to fit the top (see p. 11) and glue firmly in place. Take particular care that the edges are fixed down well to give a neat join.

Comfy Easy Chair

METHOD

1 Cut pieces from the appropriate thickness of balsa. Use the full size templates to shape them, either by cutting or sanding, or a combination of the two.

2 Glue the two seat bases together, one on top of the other to make a single base ¾in thick.

3 Glue together the back and the sides around the seat base (see plan view).

4 Cover the inside of the chair sides with fabric-covered card (see p. 11).

5 Cut fabric and card for the outsides of the chair sides, but do not turn over and glue the fabric along the back edge. Glue in place on the chair sides, wrapping the free edge of fabric to the back of the chair and gluing neatly in place.

6 Prepare padded card to fit the inside of the chair back, BUT only turn over and glue the long sides, leaving the top and bottom overlap fabric free.

7 Attach the padded card to the inside of the chair back. The overlap fabric at the bottom should be stuck to the chair base. At the top edge, snip the curved areas, apply glue and wrap the free fabric neatly over the top of the chair back, and press firmly onto the chair back, keeping the layers on the curved bits as flat as possible.

8 Cut strips of card to fit from the chair back, along the top of the chair arms and down the front of the chair sides (about 3½in long x ⁵⁄₁₆in wide)

9 You now need fabric strips 3 times the width of these and about ¾in longer, plus a strip of thin wadding the same width as the card. Attach this to the card. With the wrong side of the fabric facing, position the padding and card (padding next to the

fabric), in the centre of the fabric strip. Glue the fabric either side of the central padded strip and fold over – first one side and then the other, pressing firmly to the card to stick it in place.

10 Glue the padded arm strips in place, holding firmly against the chair until the glue dries. The top end should tuck under the edge of the back fabric. At the lower end, remove any padding that is beyond the bottom edge of the chair side, add a little extra glue to the inside of the folded fabric, and glue this end to the bottom of the chair, as flat as possible.

11 Now prepare a piece of covered card for the back of the chair, and glue in place to cover up the turned over fabric edges and any loose ends.

12 If you do not want to add any feet, just prepare a piece of covered card for the bottom of the chair and glue in place or cut a piece of felt to size and glue this on instead. For feet, use square or round wooden beads, positioning the hole vertically so that it won't show. Simply glue firmly in place at each corner of the chair bottom. The round ones work best if you sand the top and bottom flat.

13 For the cushion, attach a piece of wadding to the top of the balsa, Cut a piece of fabric 2¼in wide and about 5½in long. With the wrong side of the fabric facing, place the wadding and balsa in the middle, apply glue to the bottom of the balsa cushion, wrap the edges of fabric over onto this, as if wrapping a parcel, and press firmly in place. You may need to add a little extra glue where there is more than one layer of fabric.

14 Gently ease the cushion into place – and there you have it. A small soft cushion tucked into the corner will make the chair look even more comfortably inviting. See Needlework (p. 151), for some ideas.

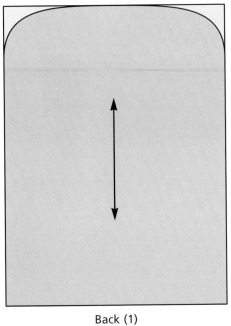

Back (1)

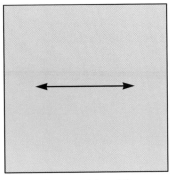

Seat cushion (1)

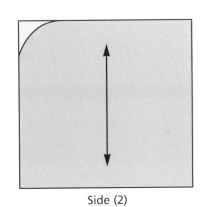

Side (2)

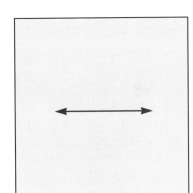

COMPONENTS

Seat base (2)

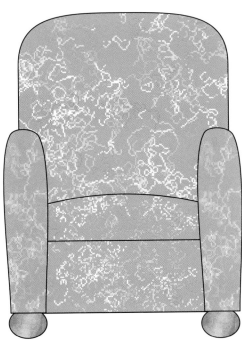

Completed assembly with optional feet
front view

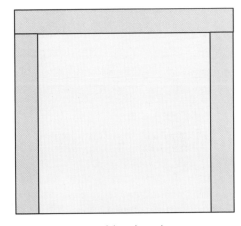

Assembly, plan view
seen from overhead

Comfy Sofa

METHOD

This is made in exactly the same way as the chair on page 14, with the same materials and tools, but with larger pieces.

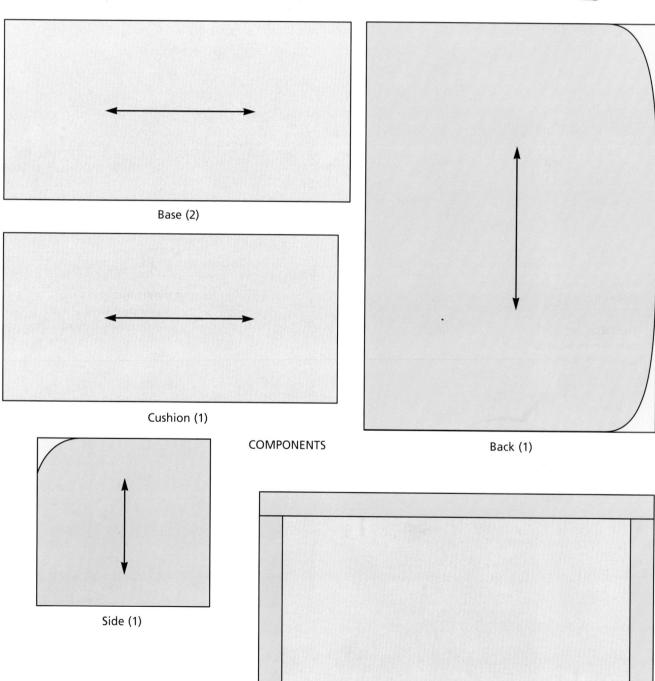

Base (2)

Cushion (1)

COMPONENTS

Back (1)

Side (1)

Plan view seen from overhead

MATERIALS	TOOLS
Balsa ⅜in thick	Ruler and pencil
Fabric	Craft set
Glue	Abrasive
Dolly pegs or beads	Scissors
Synthetic wadding	
Trim of your choice	

Footstool with Bun Feet

The bun feet on the original were made from the rounded tops cut from four dollypegs. The alternative shown uses wooden beads, about ⅜in diameter, filed flat on the ends where the holes are, and stuck to the base as feet.

Home-made plait braid was used as trim (see p. 151).

METHOD

1 Cut the base block of balsa.

2 Glue the feet to the block of balsa, positioning them close to each corner.

3 For the padding, cut a piece of thin foam or synthetic wadding to fit the stool top.

4 Cut a piece of fabric 2¼ x 2½in.

5 Position the padding centrally on the stool, using a piece of double-sided tape to hold it in place.

6 The fabric can now be added to cover the top and over the edges of all four sides. When you are satisfied with the positioning, trim off the excess fabric.

Tip: Use dressmakers' pins to hold it in place temporarily: the balsa should be soft enough to let you push the pins in fairly easily.

7 Glue the edges of the fabric to the stool sides, arranging the corners as neatly as possible. Add an elastic band, or something similar, to hold it in place until the glue dries. If you use pins at this stage, make sure that they are rustless, so that the fabric does not become marked.

8 Finally, add some form of trimming around the bottom edge of the fabric covering. I used a plait made from three shades of embroidery thread which toned with the fabric. (See p. 151 for details of how to make this and other trimmings.)

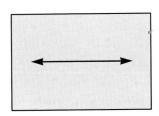

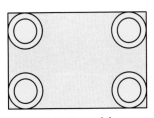

Positioning of feet

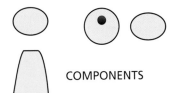

COMPONENTS

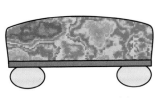
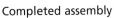

Completed assembly

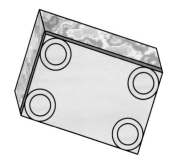

Simple Winged Chair

MATERIALS

Balsa ¼in thick and
³⁄₁₆in thick
Glue
Stain
Synthetic wadding
or foam
Fabric
Acrylic varnish

TOOLS

Ruler and pencil
Craft knife
Abrasive
Scissors

Although the chair shown in the photograph was made entirely from balsa, a much stronger one can be made if a harder wood is used. You will, however, need more than a craft knife to cut it satisfactorily.

METHOD

1 Start by marking the shapes onto balsa, and cut out carefully with a craft knife.

2 Sand the pieces to shape, giving the wings a nice comfortable shape, by rounding the curved edge on what will become the inside face of each wing.

3 Stain the legs and allow to dry, then give them a coat or two of varnish to seal them.

4 Glue the balsa wing sides to the side of the back piece. Shape and add the arm piece (see (a) and (b) on the drawing), and then glue the legs firmly and squarely to the base. This completes the main basis for the upholstery of the chair.

5 Attach a thin layer of wadding to the inside of each wing using double tape to hold it in place. Cut fabric to the template of the wing part, (c) on the drawing, allowing about ⅜in extra overlap all round. Centre the fabric over one inside wing. Glue the straight edge overlap to the inside of the chair back. Snipping the curves where necessary, turn the outside edge overlap onto the back of the chair wing and glue in place. Repeat the procedure on the other wing.

6 The arms are the next to be covered with fabric. A thin layer of wadding on top of the arm is all the padding needed. Cut the fabric a bit over-size and glue the edges to the inside of the chair back and the chair side beneath the arm, with the front edges snipped and turned over the front of the chair sides.

7 Prepare covered card for the outside of each wing (see p. 11) BUT don't turn over the back edge onto the card. Glue the covered card to the outside of each wing, turning the free edge onto the chair back and gluing in place smoothly.

8 Neaten the front of the chair sides by preparing two covered cards (b) and pressing firmly in place.

9 For the front of the chair, cut fabric wide enough to fit the width with both edges turned under. Glue in place to the chair base, over the front edge, down, and finally to the underneath of the chair.

10 Prepare padded covered card to fit the inside of the chair back, BUT do not turn over the top edge onto the card. Glue in place, with the top edge turned over onto the chair back and glued down smoothly.

11 Prepare and fix a piece of covered card for the back of the chair, turning the bottom edge under the chair, not onto the card.

12 Cut a thin layer of wadding for the seat cushion and cover the whole cushion with fabric, like wrapping a parcel.

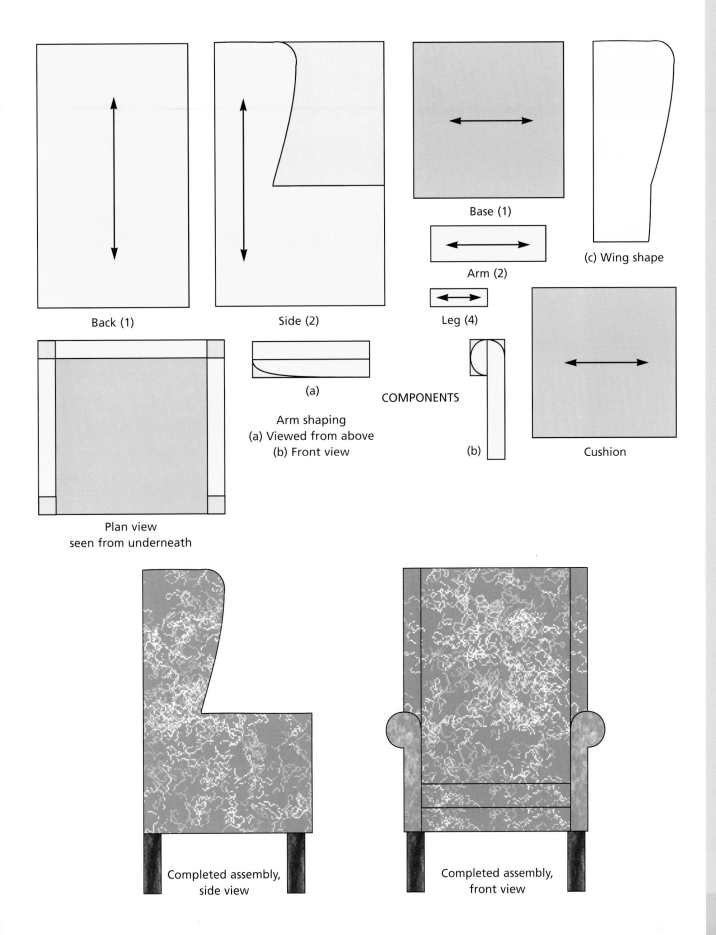

Back (1)

Side (2)

Base (1)

Arm (2)

Leg (4)

(c) Wing shape

(a)

Arm shaping
(a) Viewed from above
(b) Front view

COMPONENTS

(b)

Cushion

Plan view
seen from underneath

Completed assembly,
side view

Completed assembly,
front view

Alternative Winged Chair

This chair is trimmed with crochet chain braid and fringe (see p. 152).

METHOD

1 Mark the shapes onto balsa, cut out, and sand to shape.

2 Stain the legs and allow to dry, then give them a coat or two of varnish to seal them.

3 Glue the balsa wing-shaped sides to the back, and glue the legs firmly in place.

Tip: For a really firm fixing a short piece of cocktail stick used as a dowel between the centre of the top of each leg and the seat base works well.

4 Glue the base front in place (see plan view).

5 Glue the cushion front in place, absolutely centrally.

6–13 Pad and cover the chair in the same way as for the earlier wing chair (see p. 18, steps 5-12),

14 Add cord trim, or fringe if you prefer. One way of making a fringe is shown in the chapter Trimmings (p. 152), along with other suggestions for trimmings.

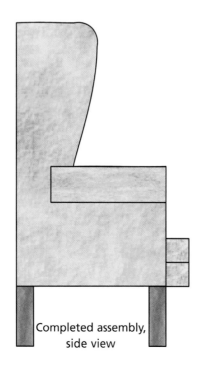

Completed assembly, side view

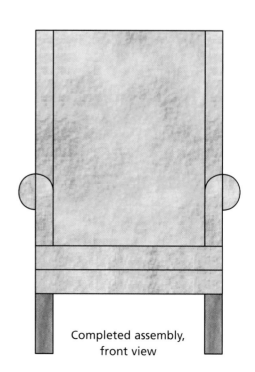

Completed assembly, front view

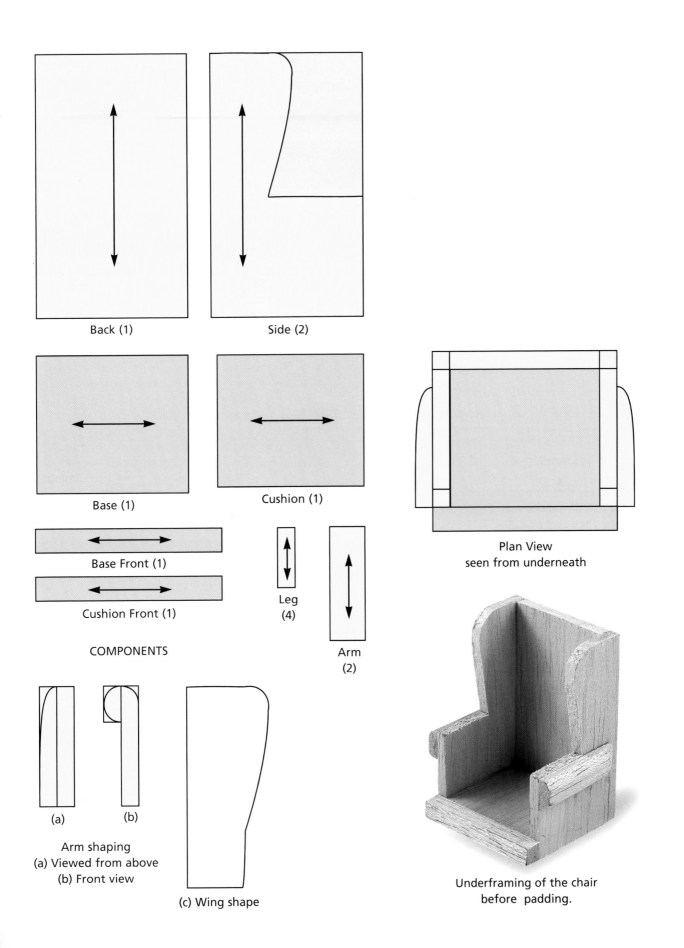

Back (1)

Side (2)

Base (1)

Cushion (1)

Base Front (1)

Cushion Front (1)

COMPONENTS

Leg
(4)

Arm
(2)

(a)

(b)

Arm shaping
(a) Viewed from above
(b) Front view

(c) Wing shape

Plan View
seen from underneath

Underframing of the chair
before padding.

Round Bedroom Chair

MATERIALS

Balsa ⅜in and 1in thick
(or 2 x ½in thick
for base)
Thin ply (¹⁄₃₂in thick)
or thick card

TOOLS

Craft set
Scissors
Sewing needle

METHOD

1 Prepare base and seat blocks as for divan (see p. 12, step 1)

2 Cover one side of the back piece with fabric in the same way as for covered card (see p. 11).

3 Cover only one half of the side of the base with fabric and a pleated valance in a similar way to that described for the divan (see p. 12, steps 4, 5 and 7). The one shown has a plain base.

4 Glue the back firmly to the other half of the base with the bottom edges flush, holding tightly until the glue sets. The outer edges of the back should lap over the edges of the covering and valance already applied.

Tip: Wide elastic bands are helpful for holding rounded items in close contact, or wind cotton tape tightly around.

5 Cover the seat block in the same way as the top of the divan (see p. 12, step 8), remembering that the circular overlaps will need to be snipped all the way round to get a neat effect.

6 Cut card for the inner back, and mark the stitching dots on one side as shown. Cover as for padded covered card (see p. 11).

7 With matching double thread, stitch through the card, wadding and covering fabric on each of the marks two or three times, taking very tiny stitches on the right side and pulling up tightly. Take the thread across the back of the card from one mark to the next.

8 Glue the finished quilted card to the inside of the chair back.

9 Glue the seat to the base, pushing tightly up to the bottom of the quilted card.

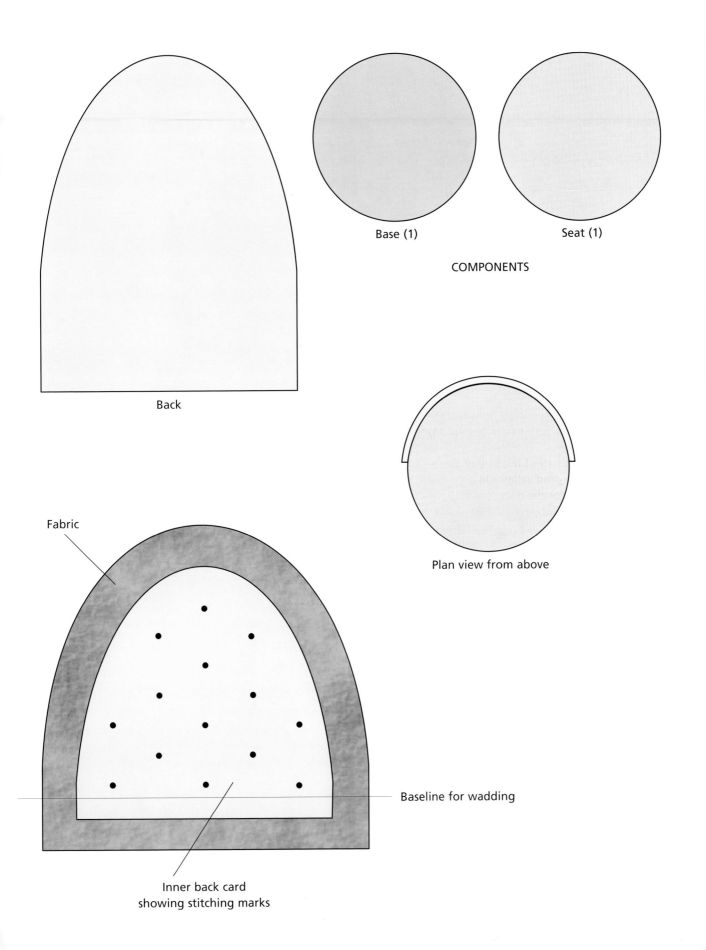

Base (1)

Seat (1)

COMPONENTS

Back

Plan view from above

Fabric

Baseline for wadding

Inner back card
showing stitching marks

Round Pouffe

MATERIALS	TOOLS
Balsa ½in thick	Craft set
Card	Scissors
Fabric and felt	Sewing needle
Glue	Abrasive
Sewing thread	
Trim	

Using a similar method to the bedroom chair, it is quite simple to produce an attractive quilted – or buttoned – effect pouffe. It serves very well as a comfortable place for dolls to put their feet up when relaxing in one of the upholstered chairs. Alternatively, what better place to sit while Granny or the nanny read a story?

METHOD

1 Cut the base pieces, gluing layers together to the correct thickness if necessary. Sand a slight radius on one face of each of the discs. Glue them together, one on top of the other (see p. 12). The slight indent all the way around the middle allows the trim to sit neatly.

2 Cut a strip of fabric 1½in wide, long enough to wrap around the base, plus an extra ½in for an overlap. Glue in place.

3 Cut card, wadding and fabric for the top (see p. 11). Mark the stitching dots on the card. With this side of the card facing down, attach the layer of wadding with double-sided tape.

4 Place the fabric centrally over the top and use a few pins to hold it in place temporarily. Stitch through the card, wadding and fabric on the marks, using two or three tiny stitches, one over the other, and pulling up tight. Take the thread from one mark to the next across the back of the card. Finish off securely after the last stitch. Remove any pins.

5 Turn the quilted card over. Apply glue to the overlapping fabric, snipping the curve as you go, turn the edges over and press firmly to the card.

6 Glue the finished card to the top of the base, holding firmly until the glue sets.

7 Finish off by adding a trim cord or other trim around the middle of the base, and a disc of felt to the bottom of the pouffe.

It is easy to make a square pouffe by cutting square blocks for the base, but otherwise working in the same way – using the drawings shown on the right of the facing page.

Round pouffe

Square version

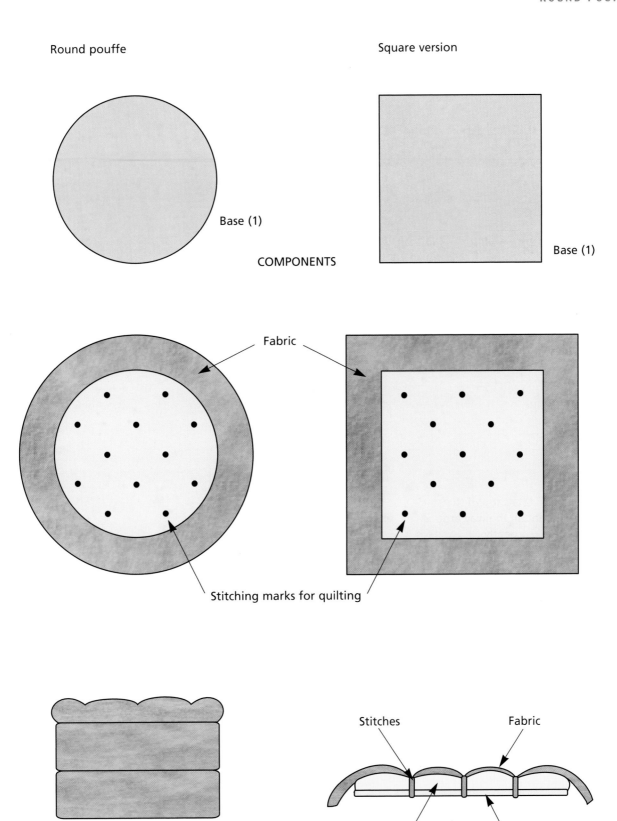

Base (1)

COMPONENTS

Base (1)

Fabric

Stitching marks for quilting

Stitches

Fabric

Wadding

Card

Completed assembly

Upholstered Chair with Piped Edging

This chair is made in the same way as the comfy easy chair (see p. 14), the only difference being the shapes of the balsa basis and the addition of piping.

Piping

For the piping I used some covered cake-decorating wires 24-gauge, and strips of a contrasting coloured fabric about ½in wide, cut on the cross. An alternative would be to use bias binding. Apply PVA glue to the fabric strip, place the wire down the centre of the strip and fold the fabric over, pressing firmly together to be as flat as possible.

METHOD

1 Cut pieces from the appropriate thickness of balsa. Use the full size templates to shape them, either by cutting or sanding, or a combination of the two.

2 Glue the two seat bases together, one on top of the other to make a single base ¾in thick.

3 Glue together the back and the sides around the seat base (see plan view).

4 Cover the inside of the chair sides with fabric-covered card (see p. 11).

5 Cut fabric and card for the outsides of the chair sides, but do not turn over and glue the fabric along the back edge. Glue in place on the chair sides, wrapping the free edge of fabric to the back of the chair and gluing neatly in place.

6 Prepare piping strips long enough to fit along the top and front of each of the two chair sides, and glue in place.

7 Prepare padded-covered card to fit the inside of the chair back, and glue in place.

MATERIALS	TOOLS
Balsa ¼in and ⅜in thick	**Ruler and pencil**
Glue	**Craft knife**
Synthetic wadding	**Abrasive**
or thin foam	**Scissors**
Fabric	
Card	
Covered wire	

8 Prepare piping strips long enough to go around the edges of the chair back and glue in place.

9 Cut strips of card to fit along the top of the chair arms and down the front of the chair sides. Cut fabric for covering the card, about ½in longer than the card, and glue in place to cover the card strip.

10 Glue the arm strips in place on top of the piping, with the bottom end glued firmly to the underneath of the chair base. Hold firmly against the chair until the glue dries. The top end should tuck just under the edge of the back fabric.

11 Make a covered card strip to fit around the chair back, as in step 9 above, and glue in place on top of the piping.

12 Now prepare a piece of covered card for the back of the chair, and glue in place to cover up the turned-over fabric edges and any loose ends.

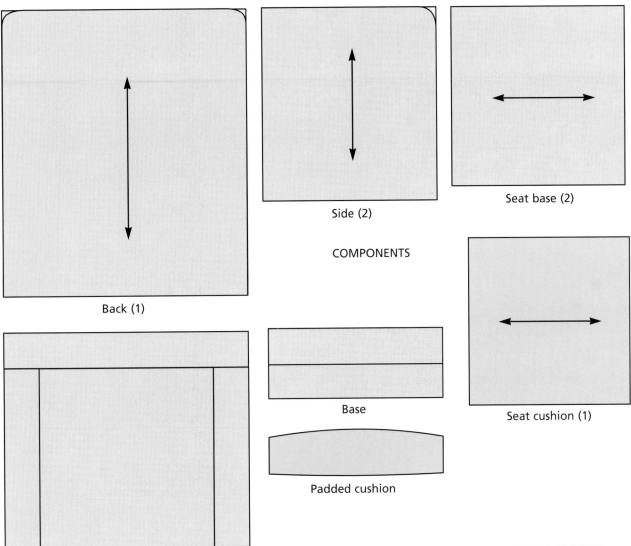

Back (1)

Side (2)

Seat base (2)

COMPONENTS

Base

Seat cushion (1)

Padded cushion

Plan view

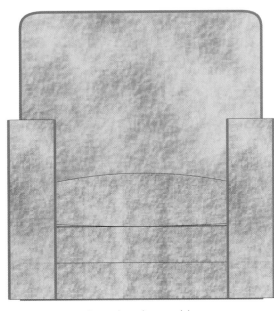

Completed assembly

13 Either prepare a piece of covered card for the bottom of the chair and glue in place, or cut a piece of felt to size and glue this on instead.

14 For the cushion, attach a piece of wadding to the top of the balsa. Cut a piece of fabric 2¼in wide and about 5½in long. With the wrong side of the fabric facing, place the wadding and balsa in the middle, apply glue to the bottom of the balsa cushion, wrap the edges of fabric over onto this (as if wrapping a parcel), and press firmly in place. You may need to add a little extra glue where there is more than one layer of fabric.

15 Gently ease the cushion into place, and the job is done.

Simply Balsa

In this section I have chosen items where the wood is evident and which are designed for outside the house. The originals were made in balsa wood. Balsa is very soft, can be crumbly, and often has a very coarse grain. This means that it will not give a fine finish, is easily marked and can prove very fragile, and it is therefore not usually recommended for dolls' house furniture. There are, however, some occasions when this wood is suitable, mainly for items which will not require a fine finish, are not to be handled much, need to be made quickly and will not necessarily be required to last long. It looks particularly convincing in a garden setting. Perhaps the following are not furniture in the strictest sense, but they offer a good way of trying out woodwork items fairly quickly – and you will end up with some pleasing results.

Although balsa was used for the originals shown, there is no reason why any other type of wood cannot be used if you choose, although you will need more than a craft knife to deal with it successfully. I chose to use balsa because it is cheap, readily available, easy to cut with a craft knife and razor saw, and somehow it looks right for a lot of garden furniture where a sawn timber finish would probably be acceptable in the real thing.

This section includes a simple garden table, a double bench seat, a picnic table, a trestle table and form – and a couple of bird tables, just for fun.

Picnic Table

MATERIALS	TOOLS
Balsa ⅛in thick	Ruler and pencil
Glue	Craft knife
Sanding sealer	Razor saw
Stain or acrylic paint	Mitre box

METHOD

1 Cut all the pieces from ⅛in thick balsa, sanding to shape as shown on the drawing by the shaded areas. If you want to use stain, do so now, and allow to dry before gluing together

2 Mark the centre of the top supports, then assemble and glue together two end frames, each consisting of two legs, a top support and a seat support. The drawing can be used as an assembly guide.

3 Lay out the top bars with all the ends in line with each other and equally spaced so that the top batten fits exactly. Glue the top batten across them exactly ½in from each end.

4 Assemble the seat bars and seat battens in a similar same way.

5 Assemble the two end frames, top and seats, gluing them together.

6 Give the whole thing a coat of sanding sealer, and sand lightly when dry. If you have not used stain, now is the time to give the picnic table a coat of acrylic paint in any colour you choose. I used terracotta.

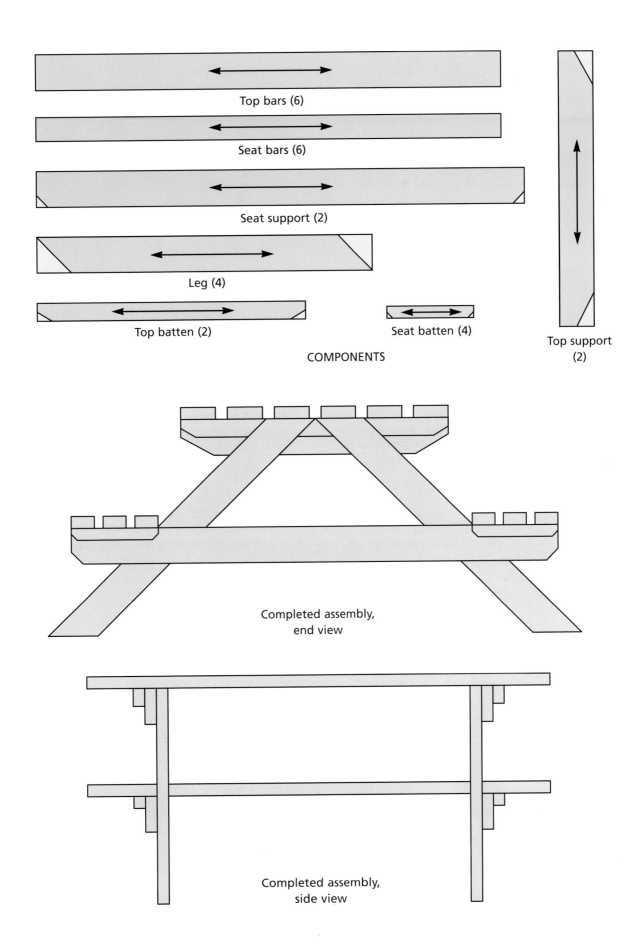

Top bars (6)

Seat bars (6)

Seat support (2)

Leg (4)

Top batten (2)

Seat batten (4)

Top support
(2)

COMPONENTS

Completed assembly,
end view

Completed assembly,
side view

Trestle Table

MATERIALS	TOOLS
Balsa ⅛in thick	Ruler and pencil
Glue	Craft knife
Sanding sealer	Razor saw
Cotton tape	Mitre box
Carpet thread	Drill
Stain or acrylic paint	Abrasive

Ideal for a picnic, setting up a market scene, or for when father is papering the parlour.

METHOD

Trestle

1 For each trestle (two are needed), cut 4 strips ⅜in wide and 2¾in long and 4 strips ⅜in wide and 2⅜in long from ⅛in thick material.

2 Glue together two shorter ones for the legs and the two longer ones for the stretchers four times over.

3 Drill through with a small drill bit to make holes for the 'rope' stretcher. I used a ¹⁄₁₆in drill bit. The location is shown as a brown circle on the drawing.

4 Cut short pieces of tape (an inch is ample), and glue between two sections as hinges as shown on side view of completed trestle.

5 Thread buttonhole thread, or similar, through the holes, and knot each side so that the thread can't pull through. The thread each side of the trestle should be the same length, to allow the legs to be spread evenly, but not too widely.

6 If you are going to use stain, do so before sealing. Apply a coat of sanding sealer, and sand smooth when this is dry. Repeat this if necessary before adding your chosen paint or, for a natural finish, a couple of coats of satin varnish.

Table Top

1 From ⅛in thick material cut 4 pieces ¾in wide and 6in long for the table top. Very slightly radius the corners, and glue together side by side to form the table top. Alternatively cut one piece 3in wide and 6in long and score for planks.

2 Cut three pieces ½in wide and 2¾in long from ⅛in thick material for battens. Glue these in place to appear to hold the planks together, and provide something to keep the trestles in place underneath. One should be positioned in the centre, and the other two inset equally from each end, as shown on table top assembly drawing.

3 Finish in the same way as for the trestle.

All you need to do now is place the table top across the two trestles, and you can start the barbecue, picnic or sale – or even get ready for papering the parlour.

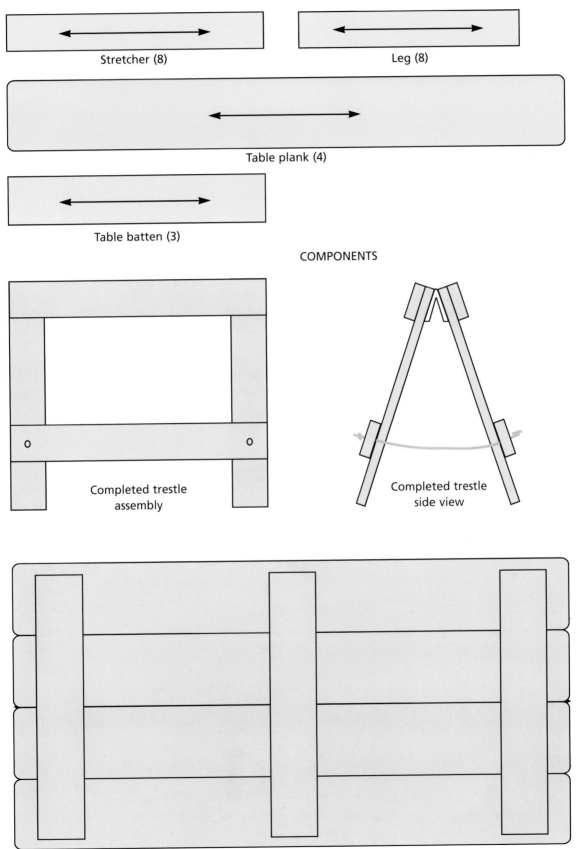

Stretcher (8)

Leg (8)

Table plank (4)

Table batten (3)

COMPONENTS

Completed trestle
assembly

Completed trestle
side view

Table top assembly

Form

MATERIALS	TOOLS
Balsa ⅛in, ³⁄₁₆in and ³⁄₃₂in thick	Ruler and pencil
Glue	Craft knife
Sanding sealer	Razor saw
Stain or acrylic paint	Mitre box
	Abrasive

METHOD

1 Cut the seat from ⅛in thick material.

2 Cut two pieces from ³⁄₃₂in thick material for the edge supports. Sand two corners of each.

3 Mark out and cut the legs to shape from ³⁄₁₆in thick material as shown. The feet can have the legs cut-out at the bottom, as shown in the drawing, or they can be left straight across. Both versions are shown in the photograph.

4 The braces are cut from ⅛in thick material, with both ends cut at a different angle, approximately 30° and 60°, as shown.

5 Glue the edge supports to the seat, flush with the edges.

6 Assemble the legs and braces to the seat, between the sides and inset equidistant from the ends. See cross section of completed assembly.

7 If you are going to use stain, do so before sealing. Apply a coat of sanding sealer, and sand smooth when this is dry. Repeat this if necessary before adding your chosen paint, or for a natural finish, a couple of coats of satin varnish.

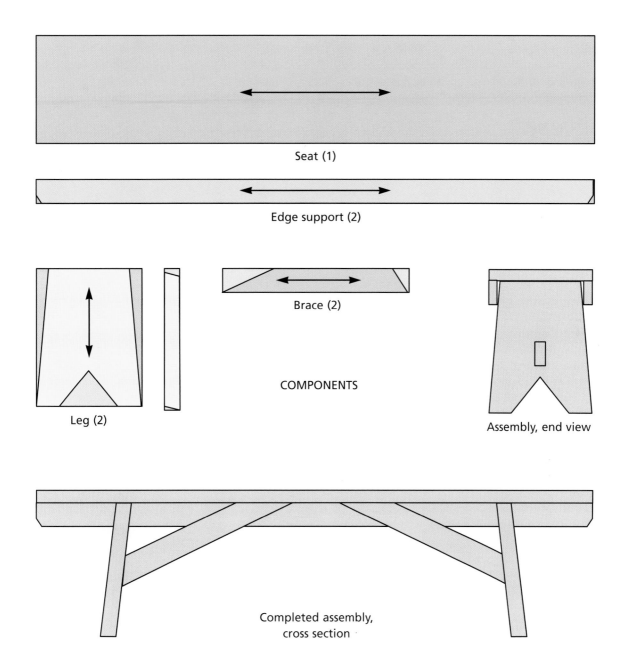

Seat (1)

Edge support (2)

Brace (2)

COMPONENTS

Leg (2)

Assembly, end view

Completed assembly,
cross section

Garden Table

MATERIALS	TOOLS
Balsa ⅛in and ¼in thick	Ruler and pencil
Glue	Craft knife
Sanding sealer	Razor saw
Stain or acrylic paint	Mitre box
	Abrasive

METHOD

1 Cut all the components, using the components drawing as a template. If you are going to use stain, do so before starting on the assembly.

2 Each end frame is made up of two legs and two end rails. Assemble and glue together as shown on assembly drawing. The bottom of the lower end rail should be about ½in up from the bottom of the legs, and the upper end rail flush with the top of the legs. Make sure that everything is square.

3 To make up the complete frame, the side rails and the centre stay are needed. Glue the side rails flush with the outer edge of the end rails and the top of the legs, and the centre stay between the lower end rails. Check everything is square in all directions and clamp until dry.

4 Glue the slats to the top of the framework, evenly spaced, and centred. Finally add the centre rail between the two side rails, to support the middle of the table. The assembly drawing shows the completed table as viewed from underneath.

5 Apply a coat of sanding sealer, and sand smooth when this is dry. Repeat this if necessary before adding your chosen paint, or – for a natural finish – two coats of satin varnish.

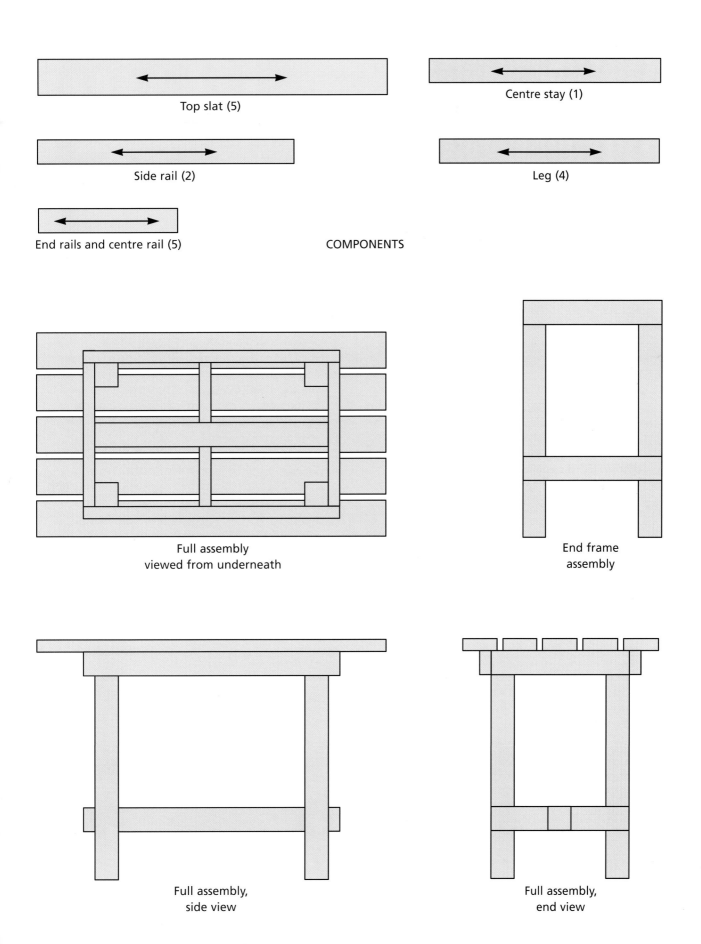

Top slat (5)

Centre stay (1)

Side rail (2)

Leg (4)

End rails and centre rail (5)

COMPONENTS

Full assembly
viewed from underneath

End frame
assembly

Full assembly,
side view

Full assembly,
end view

Garden Bench Seat

MATERIALS	TOOLS
Balsa ¼in thick and	Ruler and pencil
⅛in thick	Craft knife
Glue	Razor saw
Sanding sealer	Mitre box
Stain or acrylic paint	Abrasive

METHOD

1 Cut all the necessary components.

2 Sand the arm rests to shape. Having cut the rectangular pieces, mark one of them with the shape, sandwich the two pieces together with a tiny piece of double sided tape (your drawing facing outwards, of course), and sand both pieces together so that they will be the same.

Tip: Having cut the rectangular pieces, mark one of them with the shape, sandwich the two pieces together with a tiny bit of double-sided tape (your drawing facing outwards of course) and sand both pieces together so that they will be identical.

3 For each end frame you will need an arm rest, arm rest support, back leg, front leg and short seat bar support. Assemble and glue up the two end frames (see assembly drawing (a)). The seat bar support should be flush with the legs and the bottom of it about 1⅛in up from the bottom. The arm rest support should be fitted so that the top edge is flush with the top of the front leg and horizontally square with it as well. Glue together, checking that it stays square.

4 For the back assembly you will need upper and lower back rails and back splats. The assembly drawing (b) can be used as a template to position the splats. Do use a square to make sure that the back assembly is completely square, or it won't fit snugly. When you are happy with it, the assembly can be glued together.

5 Assemble the main seat frame by gluing the long seat bar supports and back assembly between the two end frames. The seat supports should be flush with each leg and the top edges absolutely level with the top edges of their counterparts in each end frame. The back frame assembly should be in the middle of the legs and have the top edge a bit down from the top of the back legs. Check that everything is square in all directions, then clamp together and leave to dry.

6 Complete the seat by gluing on the seat bars. The short ones should fit snugly between the legs (see assembly drawing). The long seat bars need to be evenly spaced between the short ones, their ends flush with the support rail (see assembly drawing (c)).

7 If you are going to use stain, do so before sealing. Apply a coat of sanding sealer, and sand smooth when this is dry. Repeat this if necessary before adding your chosen paint, or – for a natural finish – a couple of coats of satin varnish.

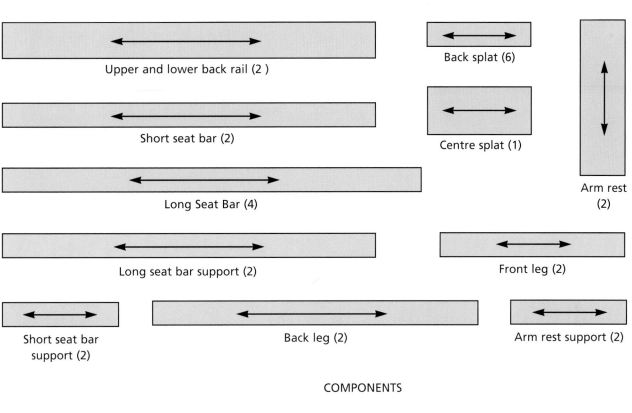

Upper and lower back rail (2)

Back splat (6)

Short seat bar (2)

Centre splat (1)

Long Seat Bar (4)

Arm rest
(2)

Long seat bar support (2)

Front leg (2)

Short seat bar
support (2)

Back leg (2)

Arm rest support (2)

COMPONENTS

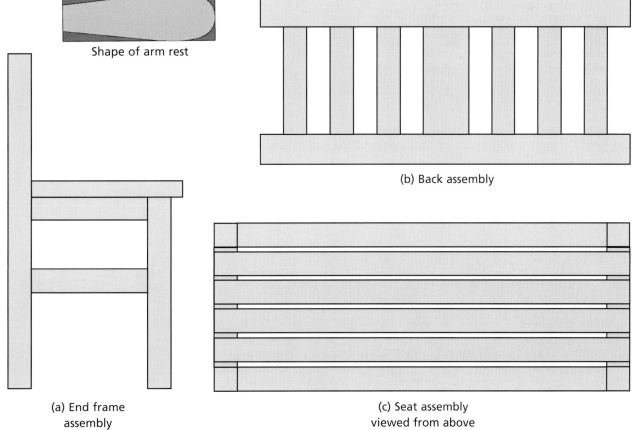

Shape of arm rest

(b) Back assembly

(a) End frame
assembly

(c) Seat assembly
viewed from above

Rectangular Bird Table

MATERIALS

Balsa ¼in, ³⁄₁₆in, ⅛in and
³⁄₃₂in thick
Model ply ¹⁄₁₆in thick
Thin ply or card
PVA wood glue
Acrylic paint (or wood
finish of your choice)

TOOLS

Ruler and pencil
Craft set
Abrasive

COMPONENTS

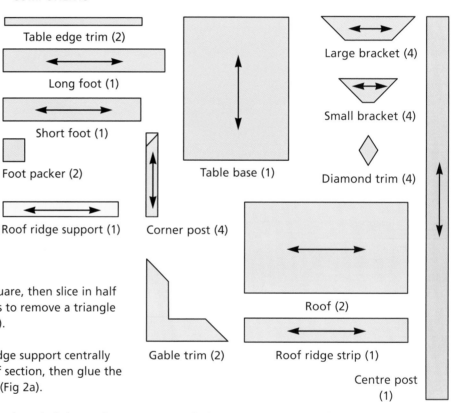

Table edge trim (2)

Long foot (1)

Short foot (1)

Foot packer (2)

Roof ridge support (1)

Corner post (4)

Table base (1)

Large bracket (4)

Small bracket (4)

Diamond trim (4)

Roof (2)

Gable trim (2)

Roof ridge strip (1)

Centre post (1)

METHOD

1 Cut all the components from balsa or ply. The ends of the brackets are all cut at a 45° angle, so using a mitre box makes this quick and easy.

Tip: For the gable ends, cut a square, then slice in half along a diagonal. Make two cuts to remove a triangle from each piece (see Fig 1, p. 43).

2 Position and glue the roof ridge support centrally along one long side of a roof section, then glue the second roof section in place, (Fig 2a).

3 Add a gable trim section to each end of the roof, gluing to the end of the ridge support and both roof sections, (Fig 2b).

4 Sand the top of the roof ridge flat, and glue a ridge trim strip in place, (Fig 2c).

5 Now for the foot pieces and packers: glue the long and short foot pieces together, absolutely centrally to each other, to form a cross. Add a packer to the underside of each end of the upper piece to level things up, (Fig 3).

6 Glue the table edge trim strips along the long sides of the table, (Fig 4).

7 Attach the centre post to the foot, gluing the brackets centrally to each of the foot pieces and the centre of each side of the post to keep it fixed in a vertical plane. I find it easier to glue this together with the table assembly upside down on the worktop, (Fig 5).

8 Glue the table to the other end of the post with the remaining brackets in a similar way, (Fig 6).

9 Assemble the roof to the table with the four corner posts, gluing the angled end of each one to the inside of the roof slope. Glue to the inside of the gable trim, then to the table and table edge trim. Make sure that everything is square, (Figs 7, 8).

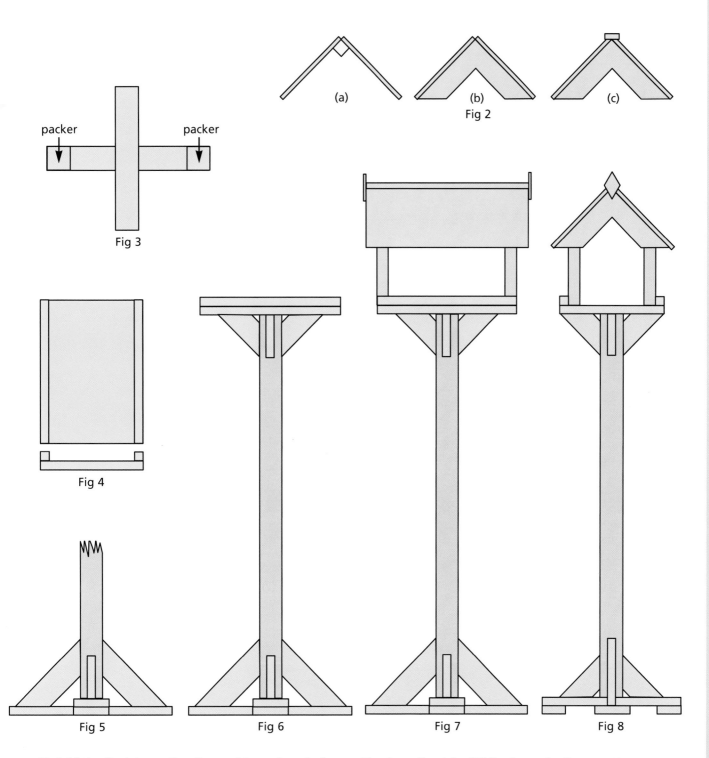

Fig 2 (a) (b) (c)

Fig 3

packer   packer

Fig 4

Fig 5   Fig 6   Fig 7   Fig 8

10 Add the final decorative diamond to each end of the roof. I cut mine from ½in ply because I happened to have some, but card would serve equally well for this small piece, (Figs 7, 8).

11 All that remains to be done now is to paint the whole thing in the colour or colours of your choice, then add some food and the birds to eat it.

Tip: A small patch of PVA glue and railway scatter material makes good bird food. Small birds can be roughly filed from odd scraps of wood and coloured with acrylic paint. Alternatively, birds could be made from one of the popular polymer clays.

Square Bird Table

MATERIALS

Balsa ¼in, ³⁄₁₆in, ⅛in and
³⁄₃₂in thick
Model ply ¹⁄₁₆in thick
PVA wood glue
Acrylic paint (or wood
finish of your choice)

TOOLS

Ruler and pencil
Craft set
Abrasive

METHOD

1   Cut all the components from balsa or ply. The ends of the brackets are all cut at a 45° angle, so using a mitre box makes this quick and easy.

Tip: For the gable ends (a), cut a square, then slice in half along a diagonal. Make two cuts to remove a triangle from each piece (see Fig. 1).

The gable trim is first cut to the outer lines, then the curvy edge is sanded to the approximate shape shown by the inner line. This is best done with both pieces sandwiched together, ensuring that they will both be the same shape.

2   Position and glue the roof ridge support centrally along one long side of a roof section, then glue the second roof section in place (b).

3   Add a gable trim section to each end of the roof, gluing to the end of the ridge support and both roof sections.

4   Glue the foot pieces together, absolutely centrally to each other, to form a cross. Add a packer to the underside of each end of the upper piece to level things up.

5   Attach the centre post to the foot, gluing the brackets centrally to each of the foot pieces and the centre of each side of the post to keep it fixed

in a vertical plane: see completed assembly (c). I find it easier to glue this together with the table assembly upside down on the worktop.

6   In a similar way, glue the table to the other end of the post with the remaining brackets.

7   Glue the trim table edge trim strips along the four edges of the table.

8   Assemble the roof to the table with the four corner posts, gluing the angled end of each one to the inside of the roof slope. Glue to the inside of the gable trim, then to the table and edge trim. Make sure that everything is square and that the corner posts are truly vertical

9   There is no diamond trim shown, but the same one that is used on the rectangular bird table (see p. 40) could be cut and added.

10 Finish off by painting the whole thing in colour or colours of your choice.

For a final touch of realism, birds and food for them to eat can be added, as suggested for the other bird table.

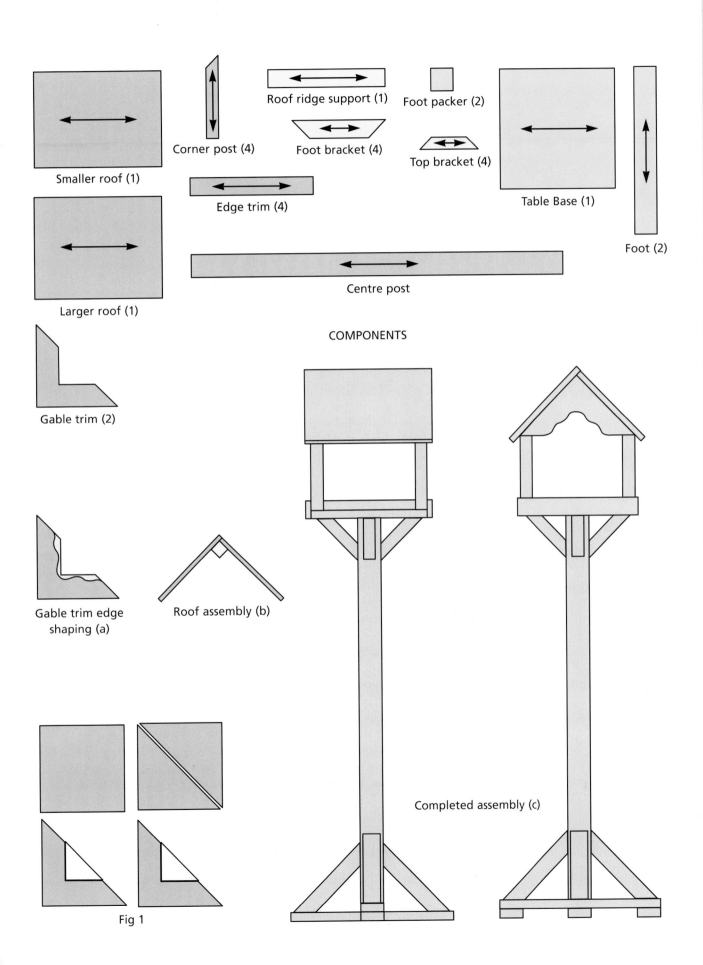

Smaller roof (1)

Corner post (4)

Roof ridge support (1)

Foot packer (2)

Table Base (1)

Foot bracket (4)

Top bracket (4)

Edge trim (4)

Foot (2)

Larger roof (1)

Centre post

COMPONENTS

Gable trim (2)

Gable trim edge shaping (a)

Roof assembly (b)

Completed assembly (c)

Fig 1

Imitation Basketwork Furniture

For inside the house there are other ways of making things where the woodwork is not of prime importance: imitation basketwork is one of them. One way to give a basketwork effect very simply and easily is to use either Aida type cross stitch fabric or embroidery canvas as a covering over a framework or simple base.

The following items for a bedroom and bathroom were made on a plywood base. I chose this because I wanted a good surface for the paint on the tops and inside the lids. The main part of each item could have been made with balsa, and just the top or lid made from ply or some other wood – or even plastic of a similar thickness.

Tall Laundry Bin

MATERIALS	TOOLS
⅛in ply or balsa	Craft set
Aida/embroidery canvas	Abrasive
Primer	Scissors
Paint	
Glue	
Cotton tape ¼in wide	
Trim	

METHOD

1 Cut all parts as shown on the drawing.

2 Glue the sides together around the base as shown on the plan view. Sand the vertical corners slightly rounded.

3 Attach the feet to the base at each corner.

4 Give all the wooden parts a coat of primer all over. When dry, sand smooth. Remove all sanding dust carefully. Another coat can be applied if needed, sanding again, then a top coat of paint. It is the top which needs to be really nicely coated: the sides will be covered by Aida or canvas.

5 Cut Aida or canvas to wrap around the sides plus about ¼in for the overlap. Glue to the sides, making the overlap as flat as possible.

6 Glue trim around the top and bottom edges. If you want to make your own trim there are some suggestions later (see page 152).

7 Cut a bit of cotton tape to serve as a hinge. Glue to the top edge and to one face of the top as shown. Add a couple of short lengths of crochet cotton or something similar if you wish to stop the lid falling back too far when open (see drawing).

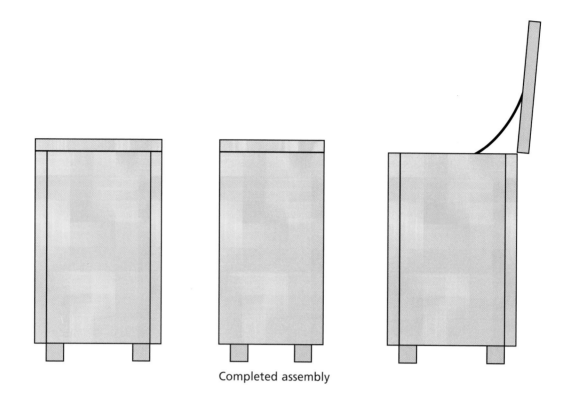

Completed assembly

COMPONENTS

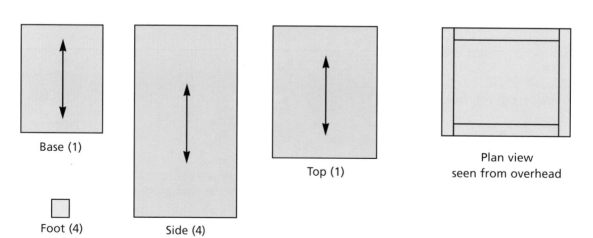

Base (1)

Foot (4)

Side (4)

Top (1)

Plan view
seen from overhead

Bathroom Laundry Bin
with Cork seat

METHOD

1–7 This is made in exactly the same way as the laundry bin (see p. 45) up to the end of step 7.

8 Cut a piece of thin sheet craft cork slightly smaller than the lid, and glue firmly in place in the centre.

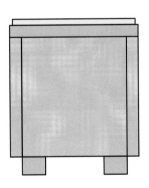 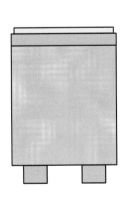 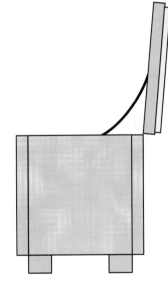

Completed assembly

Foot (4)

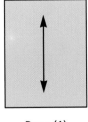

Base (1)

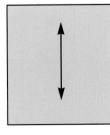

Side (4)

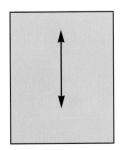

Top (1)

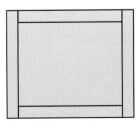

Plan view
seen from overhead

COMPONENTS

Blanket Box with Padded Top

METHOD

1–7 This is made in exactly the same way as the laundry bin (see 45) up to the end of step 7.

8 Prepare a piece of padded covered card to fit the top of the lid, and glue firmly in place.

(This project is illustrated on page 44)

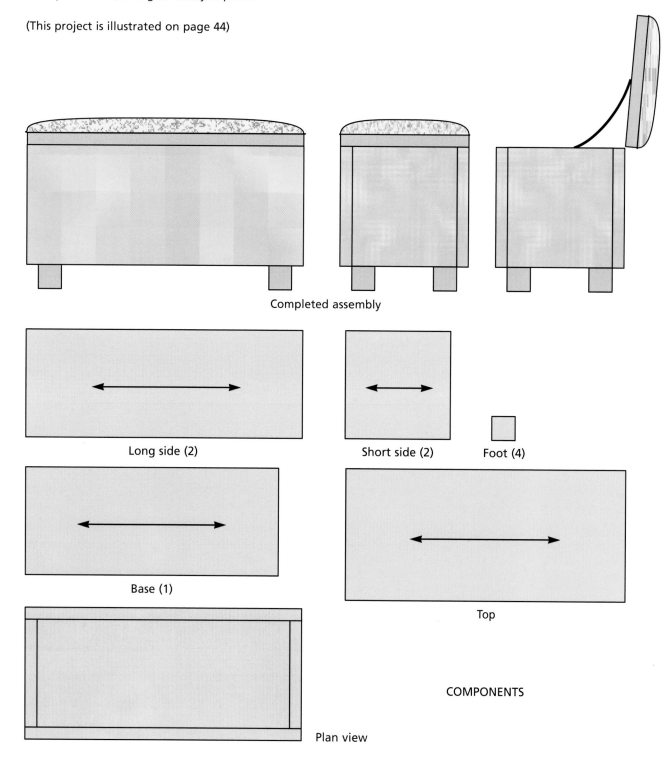

Completed assembly

Long side (2)

Short side (2)

Foot (4)

Base (1)

Top

COMPONENTS

Plan view

Basic Pieces

Now let's take a look at a few pieces which can be made quite easily from wood other than balsa, where the wood is very evident and not covered by either upholstery or imitation basketwork. These were all made using only basic hand tools, but a wider range of tools would certainly make things quicker.

Double Bed with Painted Finish

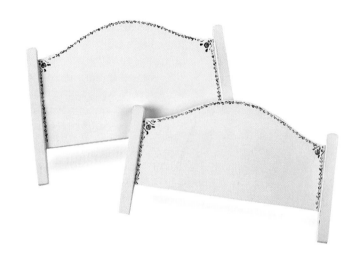

MATERIALS

Basswood ¼in square

Ply or basswood
⅛in thick

Balsa ⅜in thick

(Ply can be used for
the headboard
and footboard)

Primer and paint

Glue

TOOLS

Ruler and pencil
Craft set
Abrasive
Bar clamps

This first piece doesn't have the wood covered by fabric, but is painted. This can help to disguise minor errors, if there are any, but in any case makes a very attractive addition to a dolls' house bedroom.

METHOD

1 Cut components to size, and sand to shape as shown on the full size drawing.

2 Assemble together each of the bed ends with the headboard between the two head posts, and the footboard between the two foot posts. Make sure that they are square, an equal distance from the bottom of the posts, and in the centre of the width of the posts. Add mattress support.

3 Coat with sanding sealer, and sand lightly when dry.

4 Apply a primer coat and sand again when dry.

5 Apply the top coat and allow to dry thoroughly before attempting any decoration. A suggested design is shown to size, but if you don't fancy hand-painting your design, there are many small transfers available from specialist suppliers.

6 Cover the mattress neatly with cotton material, and glue between the headboard and footboard.

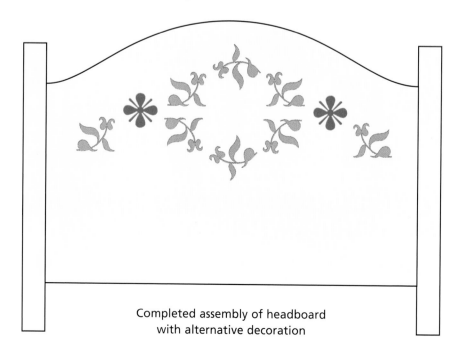

Completed assembly of headboard
with alternative decoration

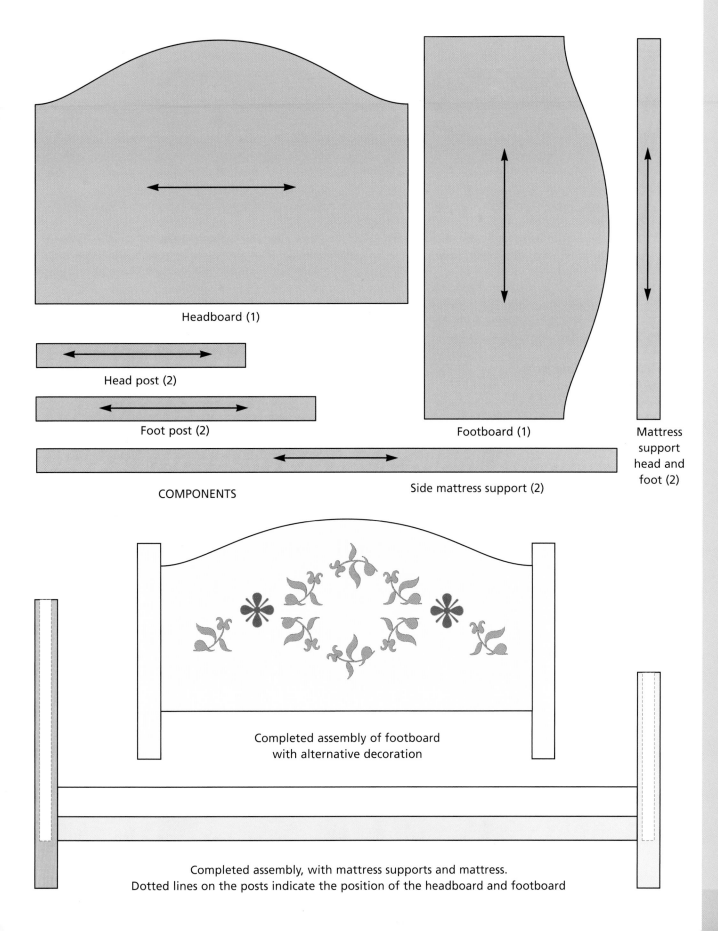

Headboard (1)

Head post (2)

Foot post (2)

COMPONENTS

Footboard (1)

Side mattress support (2)

Mattress support head and foot (2)

Completed assembly of footboard
with alternative decoration

Completed assembly, with mattress supports and mattress.
Dotted lines on the posts indicate the position of the headboard and footboard

Simple Table

MATERIALS	TOOLS
Obeche or basswood	Ruler and pencil
¼in x ¼in square	Craft set
and ⅛in thick	Abrasive
Glue	Bar clamps

METHOD

1 I find it easiest to assemble two sides first, each made up of two legs and a side frame.

2 Join these together with the front and back frame to make a complete table frame. Make sure at each stage that everything is square before leaving it for the glue to dry.

3 All that remains to be done to finish the construction is to add the table top. Actually, I find it easier to add the frame, upside down, to the centre of the table top flat on the work surface.

4 How the table is finished is a matter of personal choice. There are so many good products on the market nowadays: make your choice and follow the manufacturers' instructions.

Note: A half-size version (50%), which would be correct for 1:24 scale, makes a nice, easy coffee table for 1:12 scale. Using the same framework a variety of tables can be made. Just change the size and shape of the top.

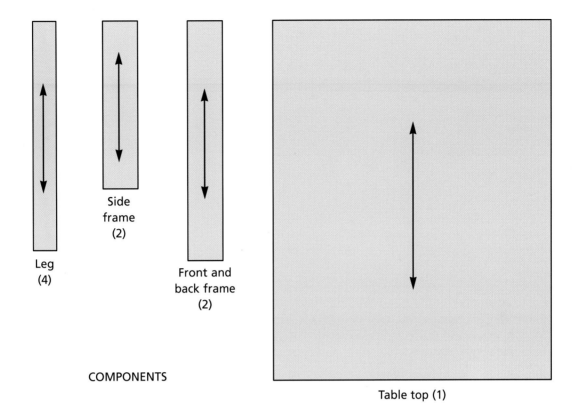

COMPONENTS

Leg
(4)

Side
frame
(2)

Front and
back frame
(2)

Table top (1)

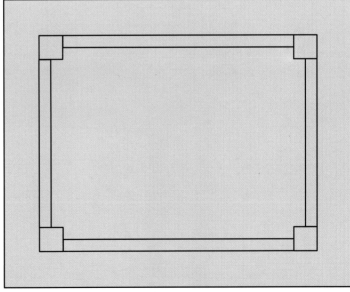

Plan view as seen from underneath

Side Table with Shelf

MATERIALS

Obeche or basswood
³⁄₃₂in and ⅛in thick
and ⅛in square
Primer and paint/stain
and varnish
Glue

TOOLS

Ruler and pencil
Craft set
Abrasive
Bar clamps

METHOD

1 Cut the components from obeche or other wood of your choice. For the lower top and shelf, first cut a rectangle, then remove a ⅛ x ⅛in square from each corner. This must be done as accurately as possible if the legs are to fit well and the whole thing hold together firmly and squarely.

2 If you are going to stain your table, apply the stain now and leave until dry.

3 Assemble the lower top, shelf and the four legs (see plan view). The shelf should be exactly the

same distance from the bottom of each leg, and the tops of all four legs must be flush with the top surface of the lower top. Clamp together, check that everything is completely square and leave for the glue to dry.

4 Glue the assembly to the top, making sure that it is exactly centred.

5 Sand lightly, remove all traces of sanding dust and apply the final finish of your choice.

This version of the table
was made in walnut.

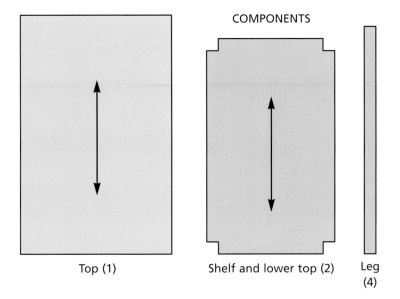

COMPONENTS

Top (1)

Shelf and lower top (2)

Leg
(4)

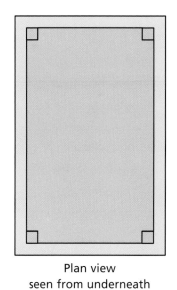

Plan view
seen from underneath

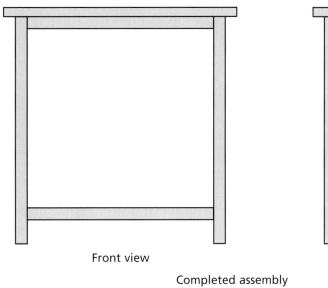

Front view

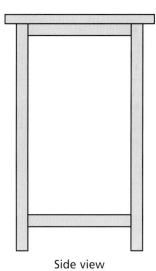

Side view

Completed assembly

Semi-Circular Side Table

MATERIALS	TOOLS
Balsa ¼in thick	Ruler and pencil
Wood ³⁄₁₆ square	Craft set
Wood or ply ¹⁄₁₆in thick	Abrasive
Model ply ¹⁄₆₄in thick	File
Glue	Pair of compasses
Sanding sealer	
Stain	
Varnish	

METHOD

1 Cut upper top, lower top and legs, using the drawing. The curve of the tops can be marked out accurately using a pair of compasses set to 1½in radius for the lower top and 1⅜in radius for the upper top.

2 Mark and cut or file out the cut-outs for the legs. Don't be too enthusiastic with this: they should be big enough to take the ³⁄₁₆in square of the legs, preferably as a tight fit.

3 Sand all four sides of each leg to a taper, starting ⅜in from one end (see drawing).

4 Stain the upper top, legs and fascia strips so that they all match.

5 Glue the legs into the four recesses in the lower top, with their tops flush with the top of the lower top.

6 Very carefully sand around the curved face of the lower top and the top of the legs so that they are smooth. Gently does it here!

7 Glue the fascia strips onto the lower top. The shorter one across the back, and the longer one around the curved edges. All top edges should be flush.

Tip: Wide elastic bands are useful to hold the strips in close contact with the edges of the lower top until the glue dries.

8 Now the upper top can be glued in place, carefully centred on the lower top, with the back edges flush.

9 Give everything a coat of sanding sealer and, when this is dry, sand all over very lightly with very fine grit abrasive. Remove all traces of sanding dust from all surfaces.

10 A final coat of varnish, either brushed on or better still sprayed on, will give your side table a nice finish.

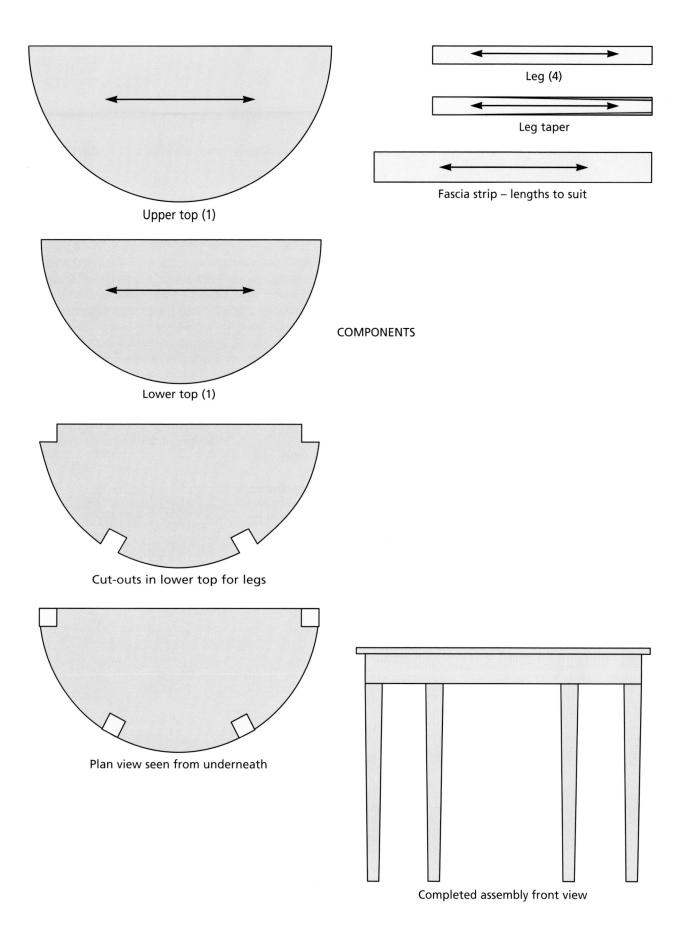

Upper top (1)

Leg (4)

Leg taper

Fascia strip – lengths to suit

COMPONENTS

Lower top (1)

Cut-outs in lower top for legs

Plan view seen from underneath

Completed assembly front view

Cabinet Furniture Construction

Having looked at some of the ways joints can be made with wood, the next logical step is to take a brief look at furniture construction.

Carcass

The term 'carcass' was usually reserved for the box-like basis of larger pieces of furniture such as wardrobes, cabinets and bureaux. Traditional English furniture makers used dovetail joints to connect the top, bottom and sides together. A back, usually panelled, was screwed into rebates to keep the whole thing square and firm. Once multi-ply of various kinds became readily available at affordable prices, it was possible to make the back all in one piece. This made things easier, quicker and more economical. It also gave a smooth surface both inside and outside, which was a great advantage when a veneered finish was required. In America and on the Continent some form of bracket was used, and the carcass ends were usually bolted between a plinth and a cornice. There is no such clear-cut distinction today, as this idea came to Britain in the nineteenth century via imported furniture, and has become common practice for 'self-assembly' or 'knock down' furniture, particularly in kitchen and bedroom units.

For the purposes of miniatures this is all a bit esoteric. The main thing that matters is that the piece of furniture looks right from the outside. In its simplest form, a carcass is basically an open box (a), preferably with a back to help keep things square and rigid (b). It may be with or without divisions, either vertical or horizontal (c) and (d). Large pieces of furniture often have corner posts for added strength (e). A piece of furniture may also have two or more carcasses (f): one above the other for a dresser, for example, or three side-by-side for a breakfront bookcase. Any number can be connected together for fitted furniture of various kinds, as has become the norm for present-day kitchens and bedrooms.

The usual method of constructing carcasses was to use framed panelling made up of stiles (vertical pieces), rails (horizontal pieces) and panels. This can, and is, done in the miniature world, but it can also be simulated to a large extent by 'planting' strips on top of a solid piece, to give the effect of the stiles, rails and panels. If rails have to be used, they are really best fitted to the stiles with mortice and tenon joints (see p. 6). However, accurate cutting and butt joints will often suffice, preferably strengthened with a dowel.

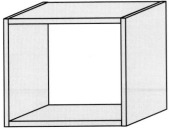

(a) Basic open carcass

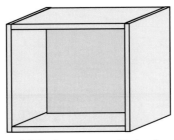

(b) Basic carcass with back added. This keeps the whole thing square and rigid.

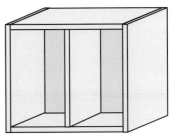

(c) Vertical division added to a basic carcass has potential for kitchen cupboards.

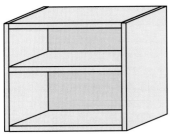

(d) Add one or more horizontal divisions and you are well on the way to a bookcase.

(e) Large carcass with corner posts for additional strength. Add another top and a door or doors and you have a wardrobe.

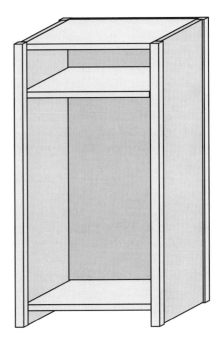

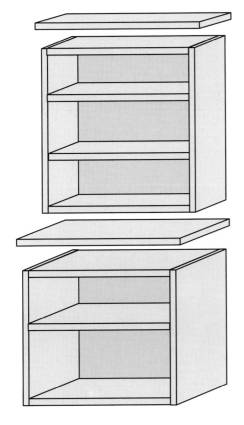

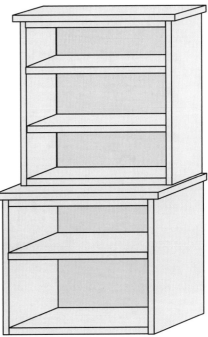

(f) Two carcasses put together with additional tops make up the basis for some larger pieces of furniture.

DOORS AND HINGES

Doors

There are many different styles of doors to furniture, depending on the size and purpose of the piece. At its simplest, for the miniaturist, this may be just a single piece of wood of the right size and thickness (see Fig 1a), cut to the correct size and hinged to a carcass in some way. Even this simple door can be enhanced by using wood with a decorative grain (see Figs 1b, c). See the plain wardrobe on p. 70 as an example.

Panelled doors were made with mortice and tenon joints, the stiles and rails being grooved to accept the inner panel. Doors can be made this way in miniature, but it is very fiddly. A simpler alternative, which gives a similar look to the outside of the door, is to 'plant' strips onto a base of a plain door. See the armoire on p.142 as an example. The material for the back of the door is usually thinner than would be used for a plain door, as the addition of strips to look like stiles and rails will increase the overall thickness. The strips need to be carefully cut and fitted if they are to look good (see Fig 2a). Just having the top rail strip a different shape can easily create very effective and different looking panelled doors (see Figs 2b, c, d). For a taller door, there was usually another rail across, either near the centre or sometimes higher. This means that for a miniature you need one extra rail the same as the others. (see Figs 3b and c). Varying the shape of just the top rail will again give attractive alternative doors (see Fig 3d). Modelmakers' plywood of some kind is often the best material for the back of these doors, because it is stable. It is also a good material for a painted finish.

Hinges

Many different styles of miniature brass hinges are available. They need to be 'let in' to the wood so that they operate properly. First lay the hinge in position and mark round carefully with a small sharp scalpel or craft knife. Then remove a very thin layer within this mark, until the hinge fits into it snugly, flush with the surface of the wood. For some applications and types of hinges it is sufficient to glue the hinge to the surface. In other cases a simple alternative is to use short pieces of cotton tape or a kind of pivot hinge, using short pieces of brass rod. The holes for the rod need to be very carefully aligned for this to work properly. It is also usually necessary to round over one edge of the wood to remove the sharp corner on the inner edge, so that the door can be opened and closed without binding on the carcass.

Fig 1a

Fig 1b

Fig 1c

Fig 2a

Fig 2b

Fig 2c

Fig 2d

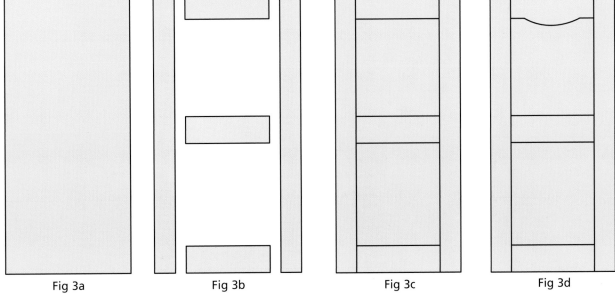

Fig 3a

Fig 3b

Fig 3c

Fig 3d

Drawers

A drawer is basically an open box which slides in and out of a piece of furniture. Sounds simple, doesn't it? However, in traditional drawer construction the sides have lap dovetail joints at the front and through dovetail joints at the back, with the bottom fitted into grooves in the sides and front. There are several different ways of dealing with the drawer front. It may finish flush with the carcass (a) or it may be set back a bit (b). A slightly larger extra piece may be added to the front of the drawer to overlap onto the carcass and cover the gap around the drawer (c), or a similar effect may be achieved from solid timber by cutting a rebate all around. Sometimes the front is made wider than the drawer itself so that it overlaps at the sides to finish flush with the carcass (d). These are shown on the drawing Drawer front arrangements, below.

Don't panic, however: I'm not going to suggest that you make drawers with dovetail joints! It is quite easy to get the same effect in miniature drawers without any fancy joints. You just need to be able to cut and glue accurately. The basic method that I use for miniature drawers is shown in stages on the drawing: Fig 1 shows the components; Fig 2 shows the arrangement of the sides, front and back around the base, where the front and back are both cut the same length; Fig 3 shows the arrangement I prefer, as it gives a little more latitude for fitting the drawer, and in any case is nearer to the 'proper' way; Fig 4 shows how these drawers fit into the carcass; Fig 5 has an additional decorative front piece, which overlaps the drawer opening all the way round; and Fig 6 has an additional decorative piece smaller than the drawer front to give a raised panel effect.

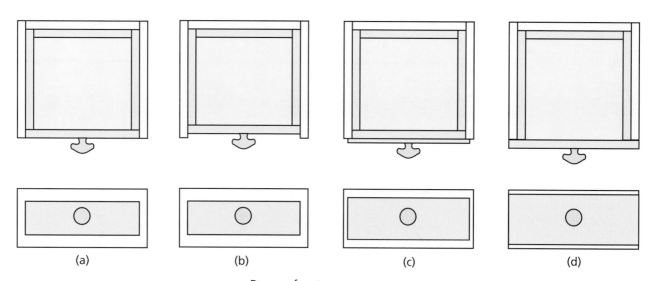

(a)   (b)   (c)   (d)

Drawer front arrangements.
The carcass is represented by the grey colour, and the drawer parts by the brown colour.

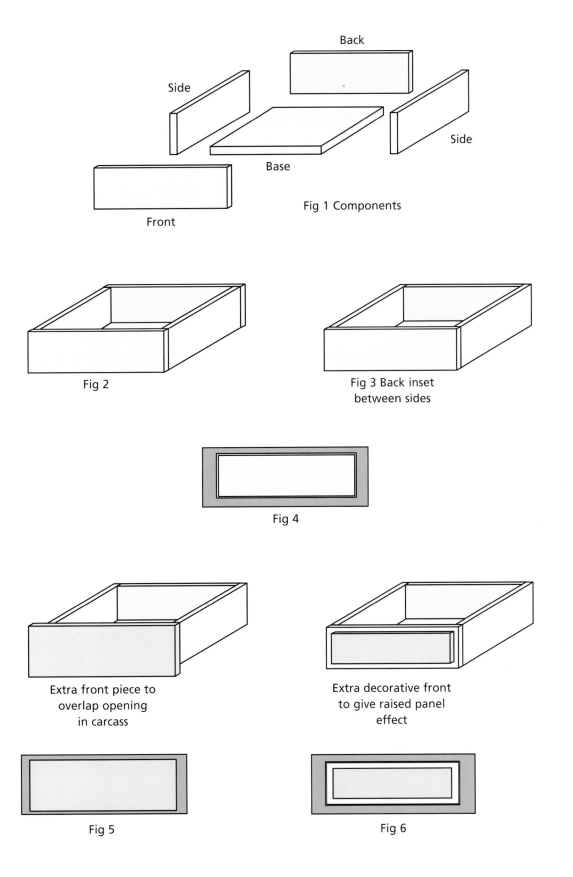

Back

Side

Side

Base

Front

Fig 1 Components

Fig 2

Fig 3 Back inset
between sides

Fig 4

Extra front piece to
overlap opening
in carcass

Extra decorative front
to give raised panel
effect

Fig 5

Fig 6

Basic Cabinet Pieces

Having discussed the various parts of furniture construction, here are some simple pieces to demonstrate how carcass construction can be used for miniature furniture

Open Display Shelves or Book Shelves

MATERIALS	TOOLS
Obeche or basswood ¼in x ¼in and ⅛in thick Primer and paint/stain and varnish (or other finish of your choice) Glue	Ruler and Pencil Craft set Abrasive Bar clamps

This is really a box, with divisions and feet, open back and front. It is made very easily if the cutting is square and accurate. For a stronger unit a back can be added (see the drawing on p. 59).

METHOD

1 Cut the components and round over one edge of each foot as shown on the drawing. Stain the wood to the colour you like (or leave to be finished with a coat of paint if you prefer).

Note: If you are making the version with the back on, the lower top, bottom and shelf need to be ¹⁄₁₆in narrower than the templates shown, to allow for the thickness of the back.

2 Assemble the sides, lower top and bottom to form an open box. Make sure that the corners are perfectly square, and that the top and bottom edges of the sides are flush with the lower top and bottom.

Note: For the version with the back on, fix the back between the two sides, with the top and bottom edges level and the back flush with the long back edge of the sides. Then glue the lower top and bottom in place.

3 Insert the shelves and glue in place. The spacing I used is shown in the cross section on the drawing. So long as you make sure they are level, the spacing can be as you wish. Do check, though, that they are even both sides and level back to front.

4 Glue the feet and upper top in place, checking that the top is nicely centred.

5 Sand lightly and finish the piece off with either varnish or polish if you have stained it. Alternatively, give it a coat of primer and a top coat, rubbing down lightly between coats, and making sure that all sanding dust is removed each time before applying the next coat.

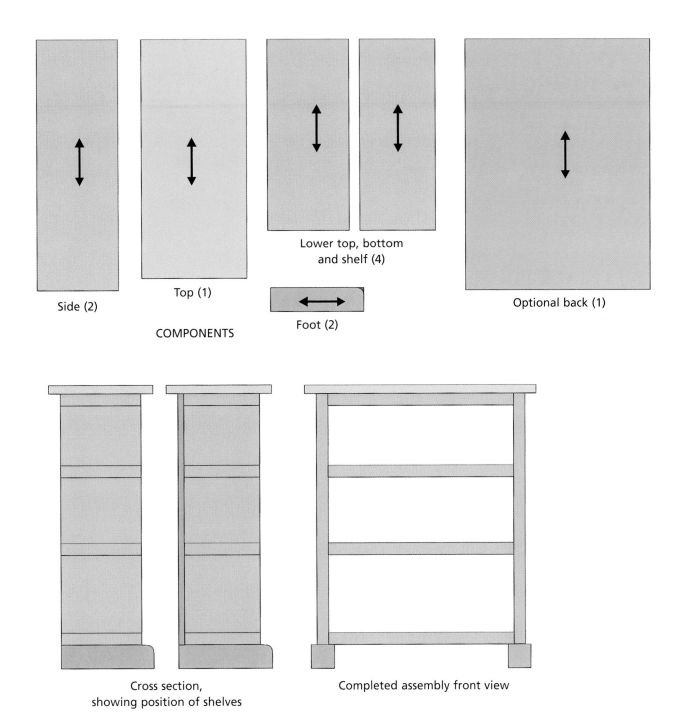

Side (2)

Top (1)

COMPONENTS

Lower top, bottom
and shelf (4)

Foot (2)

Optional back (1)

Cross section,
showing position of shelves

Completed assembly front view

Hanging Shelf

MATERIALS	TOOLS
Obeche or basswood	Ruler and pencil
³⁄₃₂in thick	Craft set
Primer and paint/stain	Needle files
and varnish (or other	Drill and drill bits
finish of your choice)	Abrasive
Glue	Bar clamps

Similar in some ways to the previous shelf unit, but this time there is no top and no feet, while a simple method of decoration is used to embellish the front.

METHOD

1 Cut out the components as shown on the drawing.

2 Sand the top edge of the back and the front edges of the sides to shape, or cut with a fretsaw.

Tip: wrap a small piece of abrasive around a piece of dowel, round pencil, plastic pen case, or something similar, and use to give the curves a nice smooth shape

3 Carefully mark the positions of the holes on the front rail (see (a) on the drawing), drill the holes, and use fine needle files to elongate the holes, as shown on the drawing (b). The decoration on the top of the back is done in a similar way.

4 If you intend to have a stained and varnished or polished finish, apply the stain now, according to the manufacturers' instructions. Assemble and glue together the back, sides shelves and front rail. The positions for the shelves are given on the vertical cross section.

5 All that remains to be done now is to give everything a light sanding, to clear away any sanding dust and to finish to your own choice.

Front view

Completed assembly

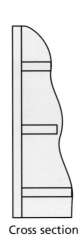

Cross section

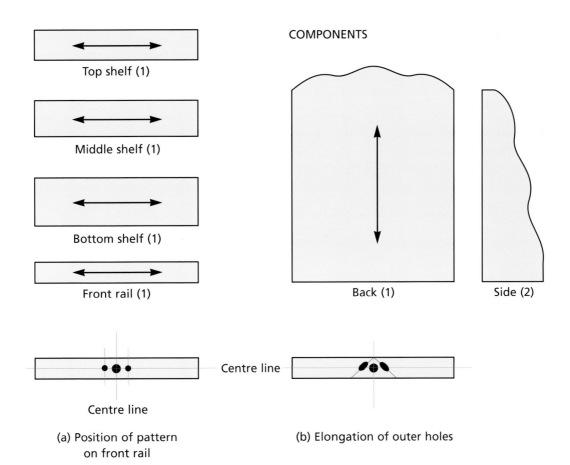

Top shelf (1)

Middle shelf (1)

Bottom shelf (1)

Front rail (1)

COMPONENTS

Back (1)

Side (2)

Centre line

Centre line

(a) Position of pattern
on front rail

(b) Elongation of outer holes

Plain Wardrobe

MATERIALS

Obeche or basswood
⅛in and ³⁄₃₂in thick
Primer and paint or
stain and varnish
(or other finish of
your choice)
Glue
Brass rod ³⁄₃₂in diam.
Hinges or brass rod
¹⁄₁₆in diam.

TOOLS

Ruler and pencil
Craft set
Drill and drill bits
Abrasive
Bar clamps

METHOD

1   Mark the components onto the relevant thickness of wood and cut out.

2   Assemble and glue together the two sides, back, top and bottom to form a box.

3   Now the shelf can be added inside the wardrobe about one inch down from the top.

4   The hanging rail supports go immediately below the shelf, with a piece of brass rod between them for a rail. Cut the rod to fit the width of the wardrobe. Glue one support in place. Apply glue to the other support, place rail in position in the fixed support, slip the second support over the end of the rod and press the glued surface firmly to the side of the wardrobe.

5   Dry-fit the doors. If you are using pivot pins, as I did, first make holes for the pins in the top and bottom of the doors. They need to be centred ¹⁄₁₆in from the back edge of the door, which should be rounded slightly. Carefully mark the positions for the pivot pin holes in the top and bottom of the wardrobe. Try the doors to make sure of the fit, then push pins through the holes in the top and bottom of the wardrobe into the holes in each door, but don't push them all the way in yet.

5   Remove the doors again. It is easier to apply the finish before the doors are fitted, so apply whatever is your chosen finish to all the pieces. When this is dry, re-fit the doors, push the pins home, and file off any superfluous metal to give a flush surface.

6   Glue the lower top and upper top in place, to give the impression of a cornice, and the plinth to the bottom. These will cover over the hinge pins.

Front view

Completed assembly

Side view

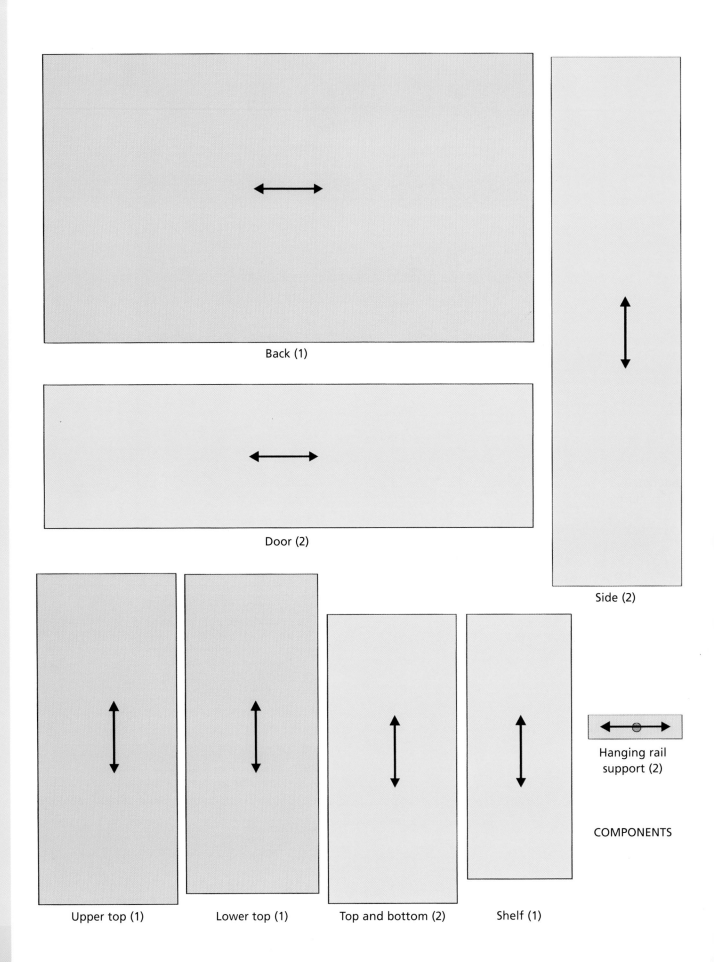

Back (1)

Door (2)

Side (2)

Upper top (1)

Lower top (1)

Top and bottom (2)

Shelf (1)

Hanging rail
support (2)

COMPONENTS

Tall Narrow Kitchen Dresser

MATERIALS	TOOLS
Basswood ⅛in thick	Ruler and pencil
Model ply ¹⁄₁₆in thick	Razor saw and
Glue	mitre box
Sanding sealer	Hand fretsaw
Paint	Abrasive
	Files
	(A powered table saw
	makes life much easier)

The original for this piece was made to fit a particular recess in a miniature kitchen, hence the sides are flush. This would make a useful addition to many a kitchen in a dolls' house, either painted, as shown here, or left with a natural wood finish. It also goes to show that cabinet sides don't have to be boringly straight. A little alteration to the front edges and the whole thing looks much more decorative.

METHOD

1   Cut out all the components from the relevant material as shown on the drawing (shaping where shown by sanding and filing), or cut the shaped pieces with a fretsaw.

2   Mark the sides for the positions of the shelves and potboard from the cross sectional view.

3   Glue together the top, bottom, two sides and back to form an open box. The back edges of the sides, top and bottom should all be flush with the back.

4   Position the shelves and potboard according to the positions marked from the cross-sectional view, and glue in place. Make sure that they are all level and square or things will roll off them.

5   Sand very lightly, then give the whole thing a coat of sanding sealer. When this is dry, sand again to give a good surface for the final coat of paint.

6   Remove all traces of sanding dust, and paint it in your chosen colour.

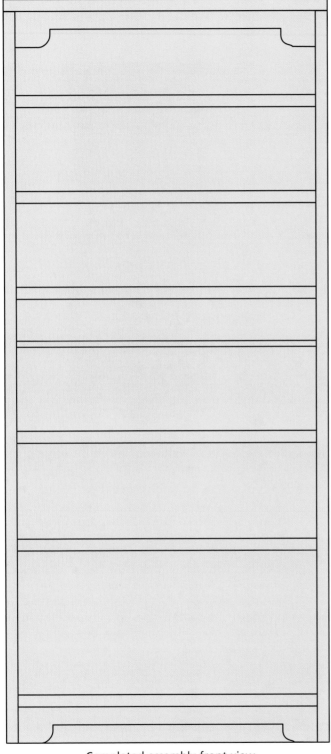

Completed assembly front view

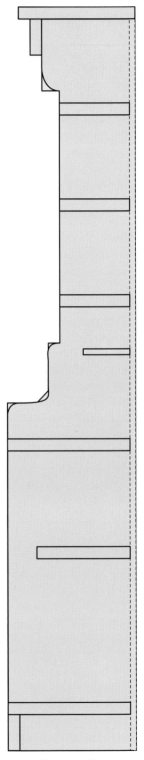

Cross section

COMPONENTS

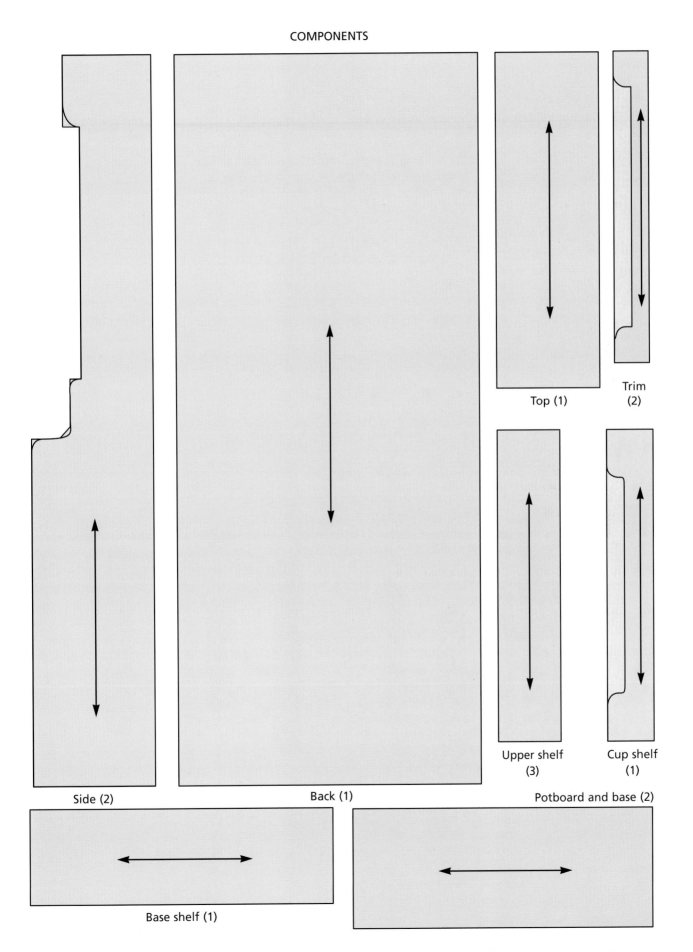

Side (2)

Back (1)

Top (1)

Trim
(2)

Upper shelf
(3)

Cup shelf
(1)

Potboard and base (2)

Base shelf (1)

Alternative Seating

There are other interesting seating methods, apart from upholstery, such as an imitation of rush seating using raffia, or imitation seagrass seating using thread. The first examples using these types of seating are purposely simple. A selection of stools with a simple framework made from square pre-cut wood section and cocktail sticks. The only tricky bit could be drilling the holes. These will need to be accurately placed for a good result.

Simple square leg framework

METHOD

1 Cut four pieces of square wood strip to length, either for the low stool or the taller stool.

2 Mark the positions for the hole centres from the relevant drawing, and drill holes of a suitable size for your cocktail stick stretchers (probably ⁵⁄₆₄in or ³⁄₃₂in), taking care not to drill right the way through the wood.

3 Shape the top of each leg by chamfering all four top edges.

4 Cut eight cocktail sticks to length, using the central portion which is not tapered.

5 Sand all the cut pieces very lightly, and remove all sanding dust

6 (OPTIONAL) Stain the wooden stool parts to the colour of your choice, following the instructions on the container, and allow to dry.

7 Glue two cocktail sticks into the matching holes between one left-hand and one right-hand leg. Check that everything is square, and that the distance between the two legs is ¾in. Leave to dry.

MATERIALS	TOOLS
Square wood section	Ruler and pencil
³⁄₁₆in x ³⁄₁₆in	Razor saw and
Cocktail sticks or	mitre box
wooden dowel	Drill and drill bit
Glue	Abrasive
Sanding sealer	Clamps
Paint or stain	
and varnish	

Assemble the other pair of legs together similarly. Light pressure from miniature clamps will help to give secure joints.

8 Use the remaining four cocktail sticks to join the two pairs of assembled legs together by gluing them into matching holes, so that there is an even distance of ¾in between the legs, and leave to dry. Clamps will again be helpful.

You now have a basic stool framework. By varying the length of the legs and the position of the lower rails, or even the number of rails used, a variety of different frames can be made quite quickly and easily.

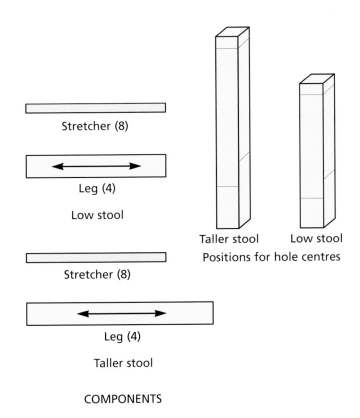

Stretcher (8)

Leg (4)

Low stool

Stretcher (8)

Leg (4)

Taller stool

COMPONENTS

Taller stool   Low stool
Positions for hole centres

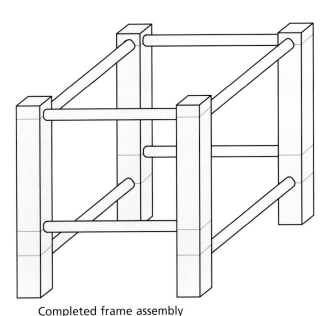

Completed frame assembly

Rush Seating

MATERIALS	TOOLS
Square frame	Bodkin or large-eyed
Natural raffia or	tapestry needle
garden raffia	

For this I suggest using garden raffia, which seems to give a realistic effect for natural rush colour. If you want to have coloured seating there is also coloured natural raffia available. To give the proper effect, it is necessary to keep twisting the raffia fairly tightly all the time as you work.

METHOD

1   Start by fastening one end of a length of raffia to one top rail with a slip knot, and tighten closely onto the rail at the left-hand side next to the top of one leg (Fig 1).

2   Wrap the raffia behind the adjacent leg, under the adjacent rail, over the top of the rail, across the frame to the opposite rail and under that rail (Fig 2).

3   Pass over the top of the rail, under the existing strand, behind the leg and under the rail on the left (Fig 3).

4   Wrap over the rail and the existing strand, across the frame and under the opposite rail (Fig 4).

5   Pass over the top of the rail and the existing strand, behind the leg and under the back rail (Fig 5).

6   Wrap over the rail and the existing strand, across the frame and under the front rail (Fig 6).

7   Pass over the top of the front rail, under the existing strand, behind the leg and under the side rail (Fig 7).

8   Wrap over the rail and the existing strand, across the frame and under the opposite side rail (Fig 8).

9   Wrap over the rail and the existing strand, behind the leg, under the existing raffia and the front rail (Fig 9). This is more or less where we came in.

10 Repeat the steps, working in a clockwise direction (Fig 10), until the whole of the top of the framework has been filled in. Keep successive rounds close up to, but not overlapping, the previous round.

11 Finish off and thread the loose end through the back of the weaving.

Note: When it is necessary to add another length of raffia, tie the new length onto the existing length in such a position that the knot is on the underside of the seating, so that the loose ends can be trimmed and tucked out of sight. As the hole in the centre of the seating starts to get smaller, a bodkin is very helpful to get the end of the raffia through the gaps.

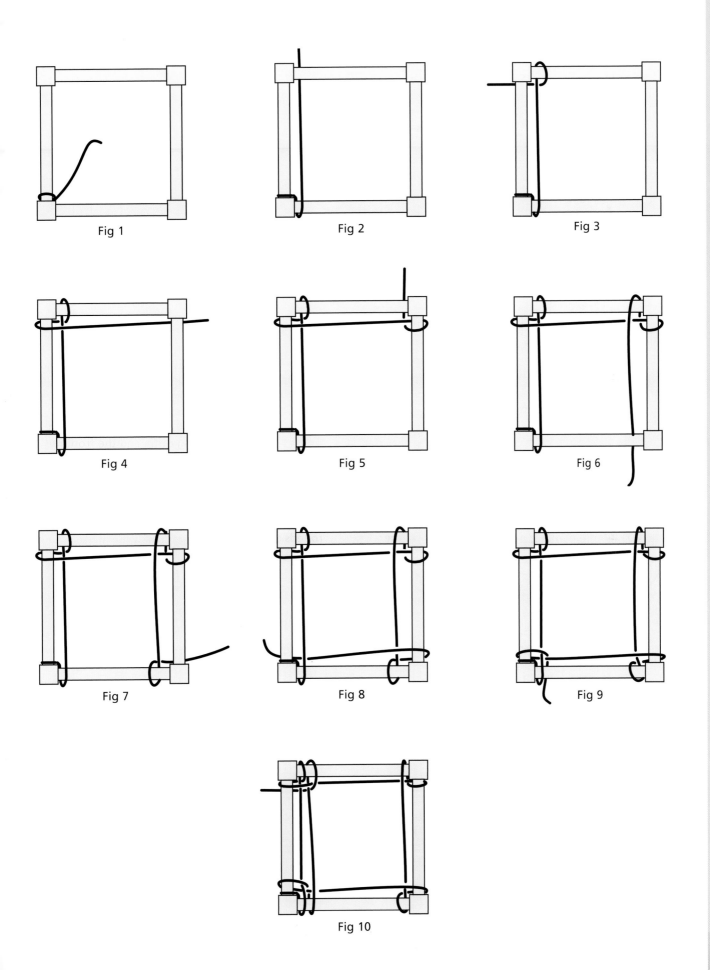

Fig 1

Fig 2

Fig 3

Fig 4

Fig 5

Fig 6

Fig 7

Fig 8

Fig 9

Fig 10

Seagrass Seating

MATERIALS	TOOLS
Square frame	Tapestry needle
Buttonhole thread or	
crochet cotton	

Buttonhole thread or crochet cotton works well for this. Some fine synthetic knitting yarns can also be used successfully, particularly if you want a coloured seat.

METHOD

1   Start by fastening one end of a long length of crochet cotton or buttonhole thread to one top rail with a slip knot, and tighten closely next to the top of one leg.

2   Wrap the cotton from one side to the other around a pair of opposite top rails, keeping each successive turn close up to the previous one, but without overlapping, until the top rails are full.

3   Take the thread behind the nearest leg and under the adjacent top-rail.

4   Working from side to side again, wrap the cotton around the remaining two top-rails, but this time weave the cotton over and under the threads already across the framework to form a pattern, before fastening off neatly and tucking the tail end of thread out of sight. A darning needle or tapestry needle to take your chosen thread will make the process of weaving under and over existing threads much easier. For a pleasing result, weave over four threads, under four threads over four threads, etc., for four complete turns around the rails, then (working under) four threads and over four thread for four turns – repeating until the rails are full. Many combinations are possible, some more effective than others. Experiment to find one that pleases you. Even more variety can be achieved by using different coloured threads.

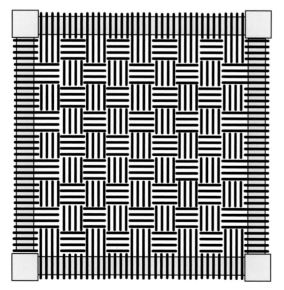

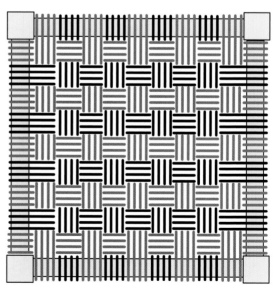

Overhead view of alternative colour combinations.

Using Ready-turned Components

There are now many ready-turned miniature parts available. The ones I use mainly are those marketed by Houseworks, from America. They are available in Britain, and give a good range. Naturally, the designs are based on American styles, which may not be strictly correct for English furniture, but there are many where the differences are so slight that it doesn't really matter. It all depends on how much of a perfectionist you are.

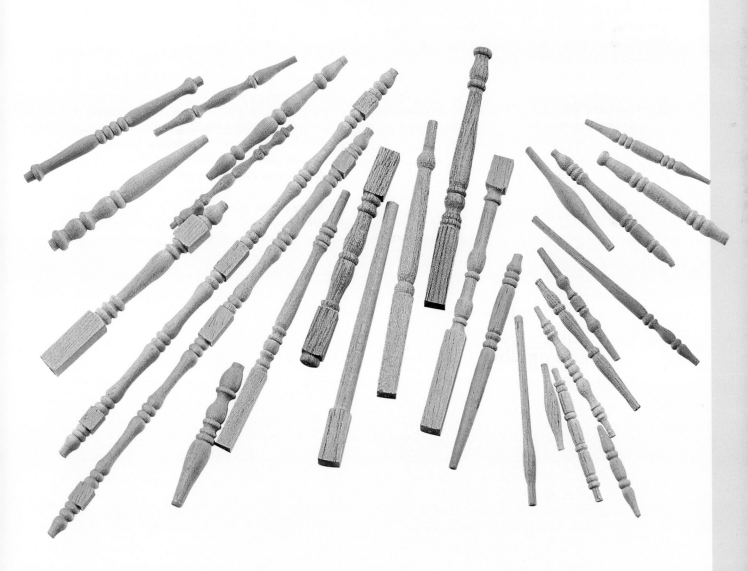

Refectory-style Table

MATERIALS

Newel posts

Wood ³⁄₁₆in and ¼in thick

Glue

Sanding sealer

Stain and varnish,

or other finish of

your choice

TOOLS

Ruler and pencil

Razor saw and mitre

Mitre box

Abrasive

Clamps

This is a simple table using pre-machined bits for the legs. The ones that I chose to use were not even supposed to be legs. They are made as staircase newel posts, but I thought they gave the necessary bulky effect for this particular piece. Using them certainly makes it simple to create this table.

METHOD

1 Cut the table top and frame as per drawing, then cut the newel posts to length for the legs.

2 Assemble two sides first, each made up of two legs, a side rail and a side frame.

3 Join these together with the end frames and end rails to make a complete table frame. Make sure at each stage that everything is square before leaving it for the glue to dry.

4 Now add the table top. I find it easier to place the table top on a firm level work surface with the bottom facing upwards. Then add the frame, upside down, to the centre of the table top. This way you can see where everything is.

5 How the table is finished is a matter of personal choice. Mine was given a wax finish using Liberon Black Bison fine paste wax finish, medium oak.

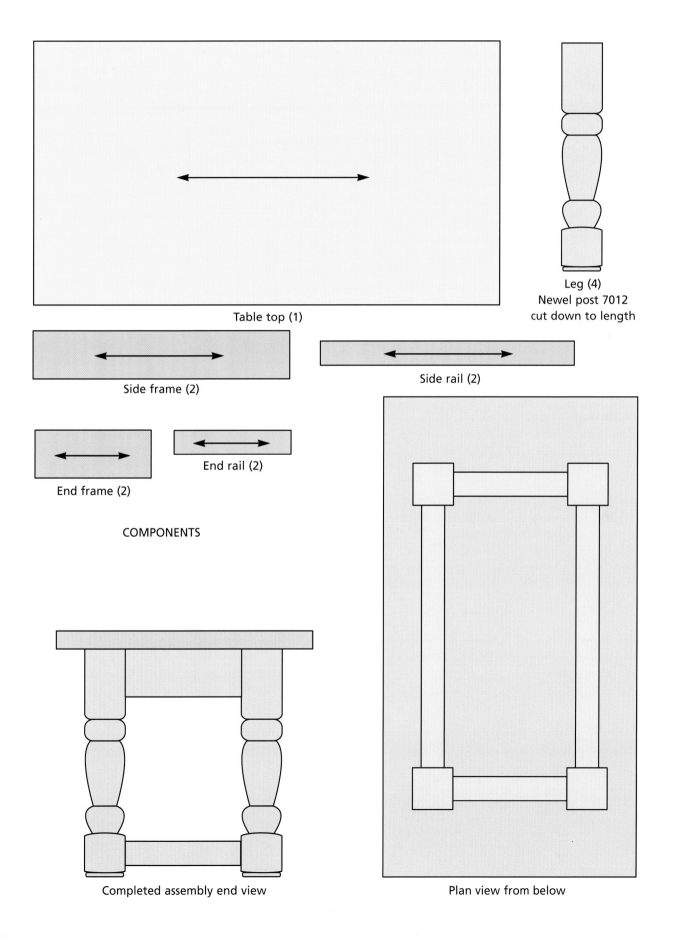

Table top (1)

Leg (4)
Newel post 7012
cut down to length

Side frame (2)

Side rail (2)

End frame (2)

End rail (2)

COMPONENTS

Completed assembly end view

Plan view from below

Small Circular Table

MATERIALS	TOOLS
Turned legs	Ruler and pencil
Pyrography plaque	Razor saw
Glue	Mitre box
Sanding sealer	Abrasive
Stain and varnish,	Clamps
or other finish of	
your choice	
Wood ³⁄₁₆in or ⅛in thick	
for alternative version	

This table makes use of ready-turned legs and a pre-cut wooden plaque approximately 3¼in diameter intended for pyrography. The only bits which need cutting are the pieces for the framework. These are all the same size, because the under-framing is square. As a bonus, the same under-framing can be used to make a square table, as shown on the drawing. For this you do not need a pre-machined plaque for the top, just a square of wood ⅛in thick.

METHOD

1 Cut the legs down to size, by removing some of the squared section at the top, so that the overall length is 2⁵⁄₁₆in. Make sure the cut is really square.

2 Cut the four side frame pieces, which are all identical. If you are going to stain the piece, do so now. French polish gives a nice finish on this table, but is done after assembly. There are not many bits to it, so this should not be too difficult.

3 Assemble the legs and side frames, as shown on the plan view. Clamp together, and check that everything is absolutely square before leaving for the glue to dry.

4 Glue the completed leg and frame assembly to the table top, centring it carefully.

5 Apply sanding sealer and, when dry, sand lightly until smooth. Then apply either the varnish or the French polish according to the manufacturers' instructions.

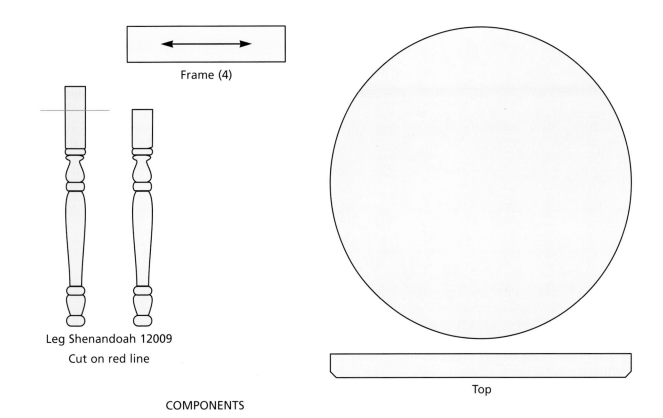

Frame (4)

Leg Shenandoah 12009

Cut on red line

COMPONENTS

Top

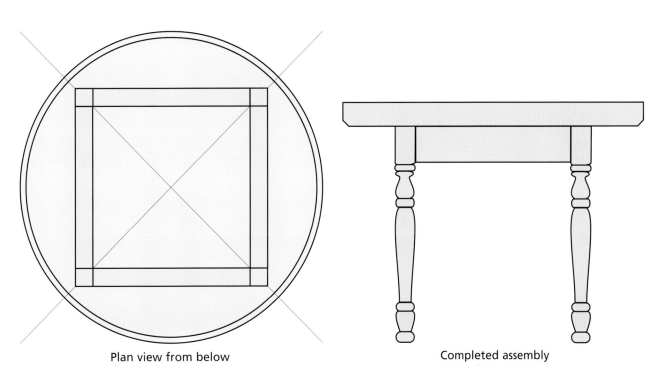

Plan view from below

Completed assembly

Square Kitchen Stool

MATERIALS	TOOLS
Turned legs	Ruler and pencil
Stretchers	Razor saw and
Wood ³⁄₁₆in thick	mitre box
Glue	Drill and drill bits
Sanding sealer	Abrasive
Stain and varnish, or	
finish of your choice	

METHOD

1 Cut the stool top, and sand the corners with a small radius.

2 Drill holes in the legs for the stretchers as shown on the drawing. Don't go right through.

3 Assemble and glue together, as shown, making sure that the stool stands level and that the legs are evenly splayed before leaving for the glue to dry.

4 Sand lightly, remove all sanding dust, then give the stool the finish of your choice. Mine had a painted seat and natural wood varnished legs and stretchers.

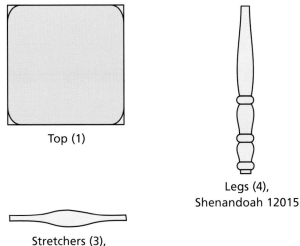

Top (1)

Stretchers (3),
Shenandoah 12030

Legs (4),
Shenandoah 12015

COMPONENTS

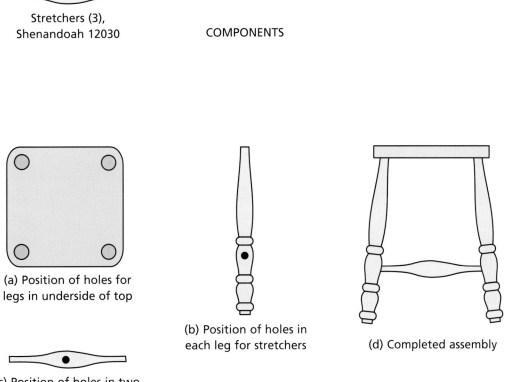

(a) Position of holes for
legs in underside of top

(b) Position of holes in
each leg for stretchers

(d) Completed assembly

(c) Position of holes in two
side stretchers to take
centre stretcher

Round Padded Top Stool

MATERIALS	TOOLS
Turned legs	Ruler and Pencil
Turned stretchers	Drill and drill bits
Wood or wheel	Fretsaw
Glue	Abrasive
Fabric	
Synthetic wadding	
Trim	
Sanding sealer	
Stain and varnish	

METHOD

1   Cut the stool top to shape – or cheat and use a 25mm diameter wooden wheel from a model shop or suppliers. (The hole in the middle won't show.)

2   Drill the holes in the top for the legs, as shown on the drawing at (a), and in legs for the stretchers, as shown on the drawing at (b)

3   Trim the stretchers to length (c), then assemble together, making sure that the legs are evenly splayed, with the stretchers horizontal. The completed assembly is shown at (d).

4   Add a small amount of synthetic wadding or foam to the stool top and cover with fabric, gluing neatly and firmly to the sides of the stool top. Don't worry about any overlaps, these are trimmed away when the glue has fully dried (e). Narrow ribbon or crochet chain braid (p. 151) glued around the sides will cover the raw edges.

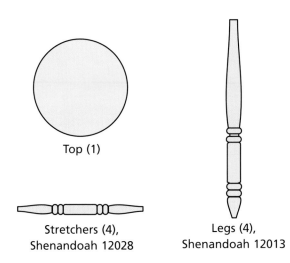

Top (1)

Stretchers (4),
Shenandoah 12028

Legs (4),
Shenandoah 12013

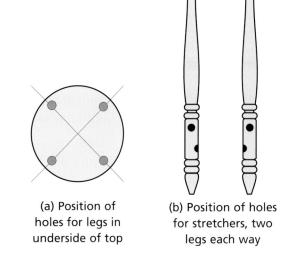

(a) Position of
holes for legs in
underside of top

(b) Position of holes
for stretchers, two
legs each way

(c) Stretcher trimmed
to length

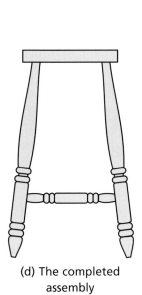

(d) The completed
assembly

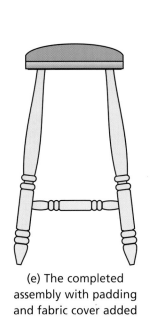

(e) The completed
assembly with padding
and fabric cover added

Rush Seat Stool with Turned Legs

MATERIALS	TOOLS
Turned legs	Ruler and pencil
Stretchers	Razor saw and
(cocktail sticks)	mitre box
Glue	Drill and drill bits
Sanding sealer	Abrasive
Stain and varnish,	Bodkin
or other finish of	
your choice	
Natural raffia	

METHOD

Make these in a similar way to the basic frame (p. 76), using the turned legs shown on the drawing, or others of suitable size. Add rush seating as described on p. 78.

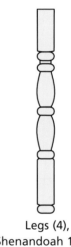

Top bars and
stretchers (8)

COMPONENTS

Legs (4),
Shenandoah 12011

(a) Hole positions for top bars and stretchers on one face of each leg.

(b) Hole positions for top bars and stretchers on adjacent faces of legs. On two legs this is the face to the left of the existing holes, and on two legs it is to the right.

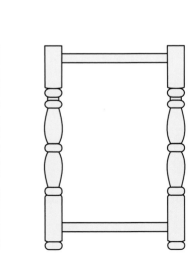

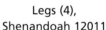

(c) Completed assembly

Upholstery Plus

Now I am going to refer back to an earlier
section on simple upholstery, but introduce a
few variations using some of the techniques
used in the intervening sections.

Fireside Chair

Completed fireside chair
with the framework shown separately below.

MATERIALS

Balsa ⅛in thick

Basswood (or other
wood of your choice)
⅛in and ³⁄₁₆in thick

Fabric

Synthetic wadding

Glue

Sanding sealer

Stain

Varnish

Dowel (cocktail stick)

TOOLS

Ruler and pencil

Craft set

Scissors

Drill and drill bit

Abrasive

METHOD

1   Cut all components and sand the armrest to shape.

2   Drill holes in two of the legs to take the dowels.

3   Unless you want a natural wood colour, stain all
    the frame pieces whatever colour you choose
    before gluing (I used antique pine).

4   Assemble and glue together the side frames, using
    a side rail – one leg with dowel hole and one
    without, plus an arm rest across the top for each
    frame. Check that all is square, then clamp and
    leave for the glue to set. A coat of varnish should
    finish the framework nicely.

5   While the glue sets, make up the seat unit. Sand an
    angle on the back edge of the seat. Glue the seat
    and back together.

6   When the glue has set, sand the bottom flat.

7   Connect the two frames together by gluing the
    front and back rails between them, ¾in up from the
    bottom of each leg, in line with the side rails. Make
    sure that everything is square and clamp until the
    glue sets. Now the upholstery can be done whilst
    waiting for the frames to set. Add a thin layer of
    padding to the seat and back. Cut one rectangle of
    fabric, about ⅜in larger all round, to fit the inside
    of the back, and another for the seat.

8   Start by gluing one end of the fabric strip to the
    back of the chair back, then carry the fabric over

the inside of the chair back, gluing the other end
to the seat and tucking firmly into the angle
between the seat and the back. Snip through the
overlapping fabric each side of the back in line
with this angle and the top of the back. Trim off
the portion of fabric overlapping the seat. Glue
the back of the remaining overlap fabric, wrap
neatly over the edges and press firmly and neatly
to the back of the chair back. Cover the seat in a
similar way, sticking the overlap to the underneath
of the seat.

9   Put the seat unit in position on the frame, so that
    the holes for the dowels are lined up with the
    centre line of the side of the back. If the dowels
    are pointed (I used cocktail sticks) they can be
    pushed through the holes into the balsa to hold
    the back in place. Touch up the end of the dowel
    to match in with the framework.

Using the same side frame assembly, it is easy to make
a matching cottage-style settee. Simply use larger
pieces for the back and seat, and longer front and
back rails.

COMPONENTS

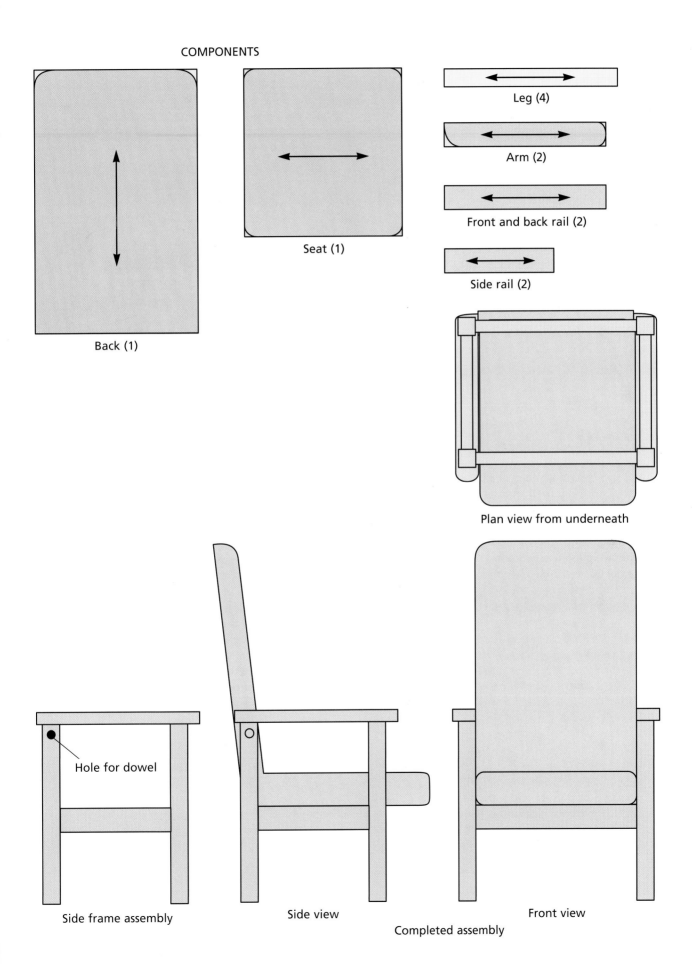

Back (1)

Seat (1)

Leg (4)

Arm (2)

Front and back rail (2)

Side rail (2)

Plan view from underneath

Hole for dowel

Side frame assembly

Side view

Front view

Completed assembly

Victorian Chaise Longue

MATERIALS

Balsa ¼in and ⅜in thick

Basswood (or other wood of your choice) ⅛in thick

¹⁄₆₄in ply or veneer

Turned parts as shown

Fabric

Synthetic wadding

Glue

Sanding sealer

Stain and varnish

Trim

TOOLS

Ruler and pencil

Craft set

Scissors

Drill and drill bit

Abrasive

This piece makes use of many things featured in earlier sections, such as ready-turned parts and an upholstered balsa base.

METHOD

1 Cut all the components to size, as shown on the full-size drawing, and sand to shape.

2 Glue the arm top to the arm, and sand to shape. Follow the sequence shown on the drawing at (a).

3 Sand an angle on one end of the base (b).

4 Assemble the arm to the base (c) on the drawing and, when the glue is dry, sand the bottom flat.

5 Shape the back rail (d) to fit the angle of the back, and round over the other end.

6 Mark the centre line of the underside of the back rail. Drill holes to take the spindles at ½in centres (e), taking care not to drill all the way through the rail.

7 Drill matching holes at ½in centres on the base.

8 Stain all the wooden bits that will show, such as the legs, spindles, front, end and arm trim, and the back edge of the base where the spindles fit.

9 Glue the back rail, spindles and base together carefully. Make sure that the back rail stays parallel to the base. That completes the framework, check with the drawing (f).

10 Prepare padded covered card to fit over the arm end neatly, and covered card to fit the outer surface of the arm end. Glue in place.

11 Cut a card for the base upholstery, to the pattern given on the drawing, then prepare as for covered-padded card. Note that only the portions which fit up to the already covered arm end and along by the spindles have the fabric turned to the back of the card. Glue firmly to the base, with the free edges of fabric glued neatly and firmly to the edges of the base, as shown.

12 Glue the legs to the base and add the trim strip, then give all exposed wooden parts a coat of acrylic lacquer.

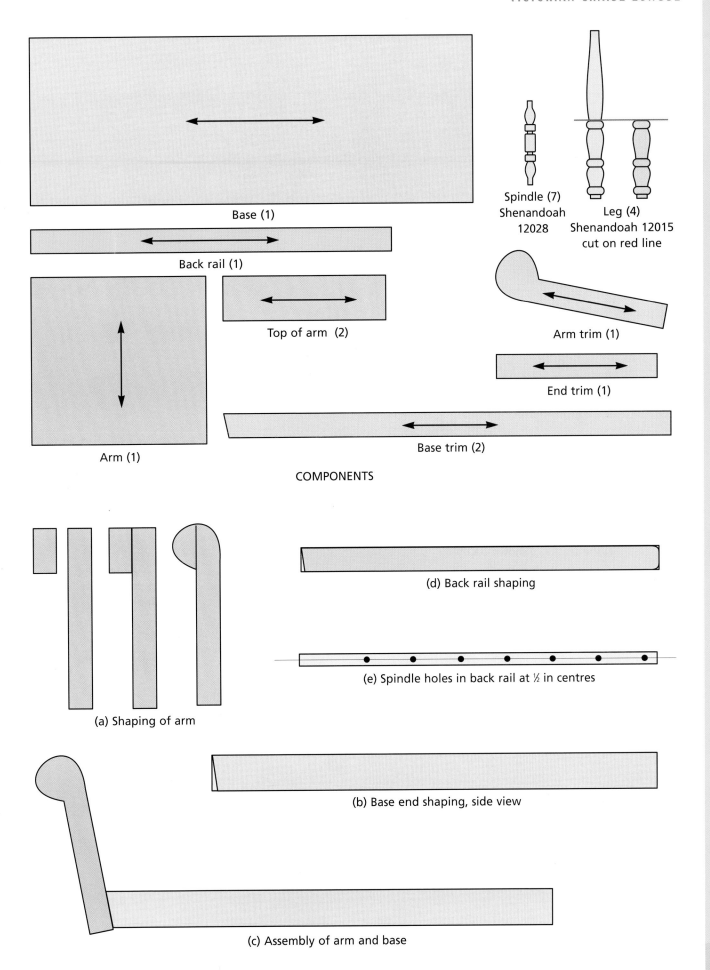

Base (1)

Back rail (1)

Top of arm (2)

Arm (1)

Spindle (7)
Shenandoah
12028

Leg (4)
Shenandoah 12015
cut on red line

Arm trim (1)

End trim (1)

Base trim (2)

COMPONENTS

(d) Back rail shaping

(e) Spindle holes in back rail at ½ in centres

(a) Shaping of arm

(b) Base end shaping, side view

(c) Assembly of arm and base

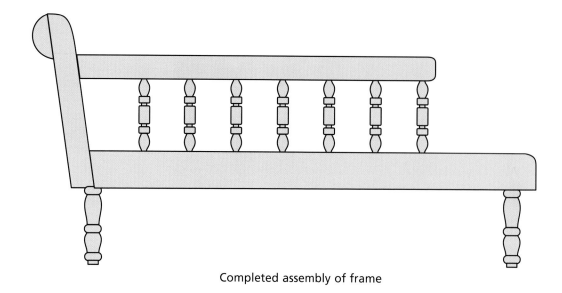

Completed assembly of frame

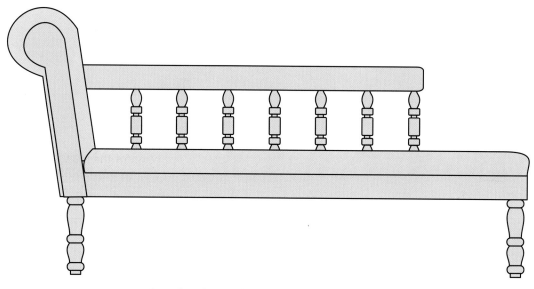

Completed assembly with padding and fabric covering

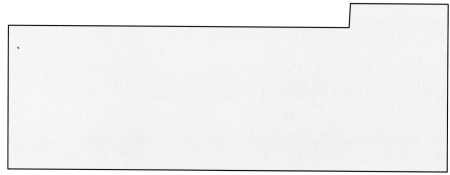

Card pattern for base upholstery

Power Tools

When it comes to power tools for the miniaturist, there are now quite a number of options available. Some work on mains 240 volt current and others work on low voltage 12–24 volt current, which means that they need to be used in conjunction with a suitable transformer. Once you have bought a transformer, however, it is relatively cheap to buy additional pieces of equipment which can be used with it.

Prices vary greatly but, as with most things, I have found that 'you gets what you pays for'. It will, of course, depend not only on how deep your pockets are, but also on how much you expect to use the chosen equipment. For light occasional use the cheaper alternatives will probably be the only cost-effective ones, and these should be more than adequate for the job.

Choosing among the available items is a matter of personal preference, finance and need, and I have limited myself to describing only those of which I have personal knowledge.

Table Saws

To get anything like consistent accurate cuts I would say that a table saw of some kind is an essential piece of equipment. The one I have used for the last fifteen years or so is a mains operated Dremel, which is unfortunately no longer available. If and when it gives out I shall have to think again!

The simplest I know of is the Minicraft one, widely available from model shops, DIY stores or, failing this, by mail order. All Minicraft tools are of the low voltage variety, and the table saw is available as a kit, complete with transformer, as are many of their other miniature power tools. This may be adequate for miniature furniture, provided that you buy pre-cut strip and don't want to rip lots of strips yourself from sheet material. It is no use for anything above ⅛in thick.

At the other end of the scale is the Minitool table saw, also low voltage. This is an excellent and robust tool, with a much greater capacity than the tiny Minicraft one. It has a rise and fall blade, which means that the height of the blade above the table surface can be adjusted. The blade can also be tilted over at an angle to the table, so that angles can easily be cut along the edge of the material. Unfortunately it is somewhat costly for occasional use, but for the serious miniature furniture maker it has to be worth putting on the 'wants' list.

If the cost of power tools seems too much to bear why not ask for one for Christmas, save up madly, or get together with some other miniaturist and buy them between you. Better still, if three or four of you get together and each buy one Minicraft tool kit, you can then swap them round between you and have a range of tools available.

Drills or Rotary Tools

I suppose these are the next most useful items of power equipment, and the choice is even greater than for table saws. Again, the ones I use mainly are the Dremel mains operated multitool, because I have had them for ages and have found them to be excellent. They have certainly stood up to some long and hard use. I am told that the later models are even better, so I shall have to save up some money again.

If you have plumped for a Minicraft table saw, then I would say that it is best to stick to one of their range of rotary tools. I went for the MB1012, a 100-watt drill, as this will also drive the lathe and router add-on mentioned below. It has a chuck rather than collets, so can take a wider range of accessories with different shank sizes. A transformer is needed, which means either another outlay, if you haven't got one already with another piece of equipment, or selecting one of the drill kits which combine a drill and transformer (and usually also provide some accessories as well).

Some useful Minicraft tools.
Clockwise from top left: disc sander, saw bench (guard removed for photograph clarity) and jigsaw. All need to be used with a proper transformer.

Drill Stands

Whichever rotary tool you choose as the motive power, to drill accurate holes a suitable drill stand is vital.

Sanders

There are several miniature disc sanders available, with sheets of abrasive that can be changed quickly because they work on a similar principle to Velcro. They can certainly remove wood a great deal faster than by hand, but for small bits there isn't enough room for fingers, and hand sanding is the preferred option for this. I must admit that this piece of equipment is not high on my list of priorities, perhaps because I have an Axminster bench and disc sander available.

There are also many variations on a theme when it comes either to attachments for use on miniature drills or to stand-alone articles, all of which claim to be the best thing for getting into tight corners and sanding irregular shapes and curves. I remain to be convinced of the benefits of one over the other. In fact I don't use one.

Jig Saws

Minicraft now make a miniature jig saw which is ideal for cutting the occasional intricate shapes and radii needed for some miniature furniture, although (as with all Minicraft tools), it will need a transformer. Dremel make an add-on which works with their multitool, but this means a lot of swapping and changing if you want both to cut shapes and drill holes when making the same piece of furniture.

Routers

These are extremely useful for making dados (housing joints) and rabbets (rebates) on the edges of pieces if you go in for 'proper' joints. For mouldings they seem to me to be a luxury, as the range of cutters available is very limited. The options of manufacturers are much the same as for other equipment. Dremel supply a router base to fit onto their multitool, which serves its purpose admirably. They also offer a router table which takes the multitool mounted underneath it. This is good for cutting rebates, etc., and is a good option for the moulding-making fans amongst you. It comes into its own, though, when cutting housing joints.

For a dedicated piece of equipment there is the Minitool plunge router – very good, as with all Minitool equipment, but expensive unless you are a totally devoted miniature woodworker. No doubt there are many more I have yet to discover.

Fret Saws/Scroll Saws

As far as I know, these are alternative names for the same piece of equipment. The range available is huge, but unless you want to go in for lots of fretwork designs for other purposes, not an essential piece of equipment at all, but very nice to have if you can afford it. You can always use a hand fret saw for the odd fine cut here and there.

USING MINIATURE POWER TOOLS

Whichever kind of power tools you decide to invest in, my experience is that they come with very minimal information about how to use them. I hope the following will rectify this for you to some extent if you are a beginner – particularly where table saws are concerned.

With all power tools, miniature or otherwise, always read and follow all the safety instructions that come with your power tool. Safety glasses and masks are also a good idea, particularly with sanders and saws. They can create an inordinate amount of mess for their size, spreading a poly-molecular layer of dust over everything in sight. Looking at this may encourage you to wear a mask when using power tools. Many of the more expensive table saws have a dust extraction facility to which you can connect a suitable vacuum cleaner in order to collect a large proportion of the dust. If you have any doubts about suitability, check with the supplier. Dust extraction is to be recommended, not only from a health point of view, but to save on cleaning up if you don't have a dedicated workroom or garden shed in which to work.

Hints for Using a Table Saw

Take special care when using saws – in particular table saws. They may be small and run on low voltage via a transformer, but the saw blade is revolving at great speed and will cut fingers just as easily, if not more easily, than wood. Never use them without the guard as supplied with the machine. When using the rip fence, the wood should be pushed through the saw using push sticks similar to those provided with full-sized saws. These are can be replaced, whereas fingers cannot. Push sticks can easily be cut from small offcuts of wood, or even plastic, but not metal. When they get a bit 'tatty' as they inevitably will, make some more. Use one to keep the wood against the rip fence and the other to push the wood through the saw. If both hands are occupied holding a push stick, there is less likelihood of getting fingers where they shouldn't be.

Cutting Wide Bits to Size

Most model wood can be bought in sheets of various thicknesses, usually from 2in to 4in wide. This is an economical way to buy it, provided that you can cut it to the sizes needed. The trouble with the wider ones is that they are too wide for the required length to be cut off on a miniature table saw. The only solution is to cut it off by hand, longer than is needed, and trim it square on the table saw.

Let's suppose that you have a 24in long sheet, 4in wide, and want a piece 4in long and 1½in wide.

1   Using a square, mark the wood sheet about 4½in from the end, and hand cut across on this line.

2   Mark a line down the length of the cut piece 2in from the edge, and hand cut on this line. You will now have a bit 4½in long and 2in wide, but not necessarily with nice square cut edges – unless you are a great deal better at hand sawing than I am.

3   If the original edge of the wood is nice and sound, use this as the datum. Otherwise take a pass through the table saw with this edge firmly against the rip fence, which should be set 1¾in from the blade.

4   Remove the rip fence and install the mitre fence.

5   With the now good square edge against the mitre fence, make a pass through the saw across the width of the piece about ¼in from one end. There should now be one nice square corner. Check with your square, just in case it isn't.

6   Measuring from these cut edges, mark the size you want. As the mitre fence is in place, it makes sense to cut across the piece first. Replace the rip fence, and cut the piece to width.

A little practice and you will soon get used to lining up the wood with the saw blade so that your cut is just where you want it.

Repeat Cuts

When a number of pieces are wanted, all exactly the same length, it is worthwhile making a length stop to guide you. This is how I do it.

1   Find a bit of square wood (about ¼ x ¼in or ⅜ x ⅜in), and cut off a length which goes across the table alongside the rip fence from the front edge to about half the distance to the blade.

2   Stick this firmly to the rip fence, level with the front edge of the table, using double-sided tape. Using this square stop instead of the rip fence on its own stops the bit being cut off from becoming jammed between the fence and the blade, or from being kicked back towards you.

3   Mark the length you want onto a spare piece of wood. Use this to set the rip fence position.

4   Hold the wood against the mitre fence so that the end of it is against the square wood stop and the line to be cut is in line with the outside edge of the saw blade.

5   Switch the saw on and move the wood through the saw with the mitre guide.

6   Switch off the saw and check that the length is correct. Make any necessary adjustments to the rip fence position to give you exactly the length you want. Then repeat steps 4 and 5 the number of times necessary to give you the pieces you want. When you have finished, you can then remove the temporary stop from the rip fence and clean off any remaining adhesive before using the rip fence for its proper purpose again.

Preventing Torn Edges when Cross-Cutting

Some types of wood are worse than others for the edge splitting or tearing at the end of a cross cut on a power saw. The way I deal with this is to use a 'sacrificial strip'. This is another piece of spare square material which is positioned on the mitre fence so that it extends across the saw table further than the saw blade. The wood to be cut is held firmly against this and is moved through the saw so that the blade cuts into the sacrificial strip. Obviously the piece of square wood has to be moved further across the table for the end to be beyond the saw blade for the next cut. Now you know why I call it a sacrificial strip: it is sacrificed to give a clean cut across the required piece of wood.

Safety Warning

Remember that the saw should ONLY be switched on when you are ready to cut, and should be switched off again immediately the cut is finished. All adjustments to the rip fence and/or mitre fence must be done with the saw switched off, and preferably disconnected from the power supply.

Types of Wood

Let's have a look at some of the different types of wood which are readily available nowadays in sizes to suit the miniaturist.

Selection of various woods. One half is coated with varnish to demonstrate how this shows up the patterns of the grain and, in some cases, the colour.

Balsa

Also known as corkwood, this comes from tropical America and is dirty white to light brown. It is extremely light and soft, with a variable grain. It is easily cut but can be susceptible to being damaged or marked.

Basswood

This wood comes from America and Canada, and is also known as American whitewood or lime. It is not the same as English lime, which comes from another species. It is fairly light and soft, and has a fine texture and close even grain, but it is not particularly strong or durable. The natural colour is greyish white to light brown, but it stains and polishes well and can be used to imitate other woods in this way.

Cherry

All cherry woods are various varieties of Prunus. The one usually available to the miniaturist is American cherry. It is fairly hard, a lovely pinky-red to ruddy-brown colour, with a wavy grain. It polishes easily, to give a beautiful, lustrous, deep pinky-brown finish.

Mahogany

This covers a multitude of different woods, all sold as mahogany. It is usually a reddish brown colour, fairly light and reasonably soft, with an interlocked grain. Hard-wearing and stable, it has been used for centuries for high-class cabinet making, giving a wonderful rich finish.

Oak

There are any number of different varieties. Again, the one usually offered in suitable sizes for miniature furniture is from America: American oak. It is easier to work with than English oak, because it is not quite as strong or hard. It is light brown in colour with silvery markings.

Obeche

This is not, as I have read in at least one book, an alternative name for basswood, but comes from a completely different tree. It is known by several names, such as African or Nigerian whitewood, abachi and samba. It has a fairly open texture, with an interlocked grain which can give a stripy effect. Being soft, light, fairly durable and stable, it is a good general purpose wood for miniature furniture. It can be worked very easily and polishes well.

Pine

This covers a large variety of softwoods from all over the world. Most are very resinous, which can give problems with clogging up of tools, but pine is mostly soft, light and stable. Use carefully selected pieces with small knots to give furniture a realistic miniature version of the full size. It can be stained or polished, and it takes a wax finish very well.

Walnut

There are various types from Europe, Asia, America and Australia, mostly light to dark brown in colour with darker markings. Beautifully figured, they have been used for centuries in cabinet making and veneering. Walnut is fairly heavy, hard and strong with a fine even grain. It is not difficult to work with, and readily polishes to a lovely finish.

Further Uses for Turned Components

Following on from the earlier introduction of ready turned components (p. 81), here are some matching pieces of bedroom furniture all using various spindles. They could be used to furnish an elegant bedroom. There are also some attractive kitchen chairs and a carving chair, none of which would look out of place in a large farmhouse style kitchen, or 'below stairs' in a mansion.

Elegant Double Bed

METHOD

1 Cut posts to length as shown on the drawing, and cut the rails.

2 Mark the hole centres for the spreaders. Start from the centre of two of the shorter rails. Mark ¼in either side of centre, and work outwards marking centres at ½in intervals on both sides of this. Drill holes, but don't go right through the wood.

3 Assemble the head end with spreaders between the two sets of holes, and the rails between the squared sections of the posts. Use the drawing as a guide, and make sure that all is square before clamping until the glue has dried.

4 File grooves in both ends of the longer rails, to fit snugly onto the rounded portions of the posts as shown on the drawing.

5 Assemble the foot end using the remaining shorter rail, one of the grooved rails and two short posts. Make sure that it is all square. Add the grooved rail to the head end the same distance from the bottom of the posts as for the foot end.

6 Cut a balsa mattress (4½in x 6½in x ½in), notching each of the four corners to fit round the posts, and glue in place. The top and sides of the mattress can be covered with fabric if you like, as shown in the photograph.

Tip: If you don't have the right thickness or width of balsa, glue layers and/or strips together to make a block the right thickness and width. If the mattress is covered with fabric the joins will never be seen.

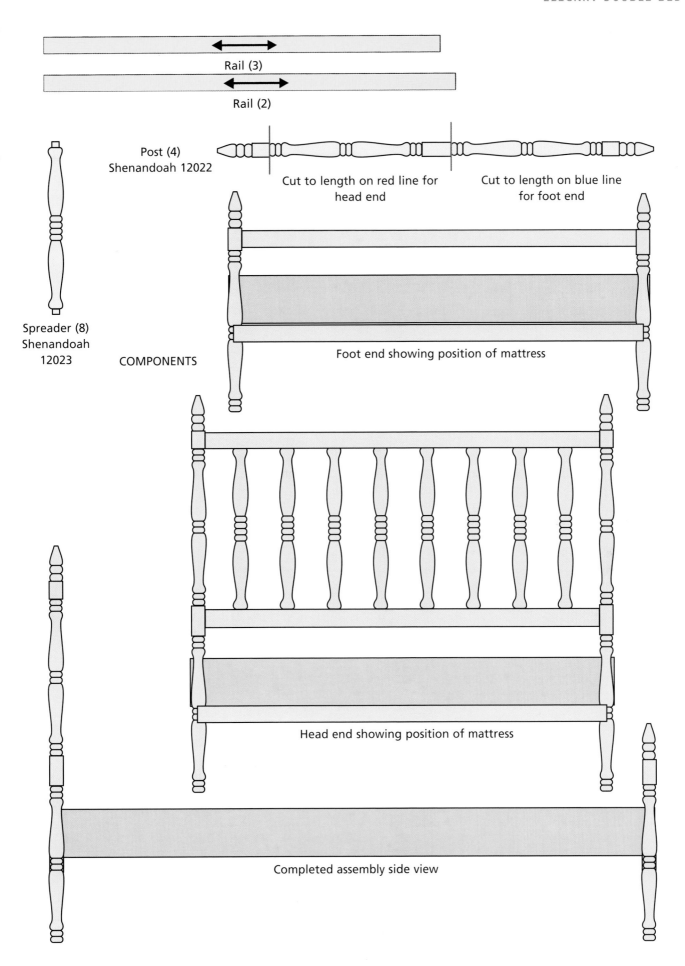

Rail (3)

Rail (2)

Post (4)
Shenandoah 12022

Cut to length on red line for
head end

Cut to length on blue line
for foot end

Spreader (8)
Shenandoah
12023

COMPONENTS

Foot end showing position of mattress

Head end showing position of mattress

Completed assembly side view

Elegant Dressing Table

MATERIALS	TOOLS
Stair spindles	Ruler and pencil
Basswood (or other	Craft set
wood of your choice)	Abrasive
⅛in and ³⁄₃₂in thick	Clamps
Glue	
Sanding sealer	
Primer and paint/	
stain and varnish	
Knobs	

METHOD

1 Cut all components to size as shown on the drawing.

2 Make up the two end frames, using two legs and a side for each frame, setting the tops of the legs flush with the top edge of the side. Everything must be square, and the surfaces flush. Sand lightly if needed.

3 Sand the edges of the top to a very slight radius to neaten them.

4 Assemble and glue together the main framework on a flat, smooth surface, as shown in the carcass assembly drawing. You will need the two end frames, back, front rail, two drawer shelves, two corner posts and the remaining two sides. Check that everything is perfectly square all round before leaving to dry, preferably lightly clamped.

Tip: A photocopy of the plan view may be a useful assembly aid. Glue this to a smooth flat scrap piece, and assemble on top of it.

5 Make up the two drawers, shown in plan view on the drawing. Clamp together lightly, check that all is square, then leave to dry. When dry, sand lightly and check for size.

6 Add the final drawer shelves to the carcass, using the drawers to check the spacing.

7 Make tiny holes in the centre of each drawer front for the knobs, but don't fix the knobs yet unless you want them to be painted.

8 Check that the drawers fit properly and work smoothly.

Tip: I use a large-headed dressmakers' pin through this hole from the INSIDE of the drawer, so that the drawer will not get irretrievably stuck in the drawer space.

9 Sand very lightly – and I mean lightly, virtually just wiping the surfaces with very fine abrasive. Remove all sanding dust carefully, and give the outsides of the pieces a coat of primer.

10 When the paint is thoroughly dry, smooth the surfaces with very fine abrasive (I use 1200 grit wet and dry). Again remove all sanding dust thoroughly, and give the pieces a top coat.

11 All that remains now is to double check that the drawers still fit smoothly (this is where those pins come in handy again to get the drawers out), sanding very carefully if they don't – preferably on the sides and base of the drawers. When you are happy with the fit, remove the pins and fix the knobs in place.

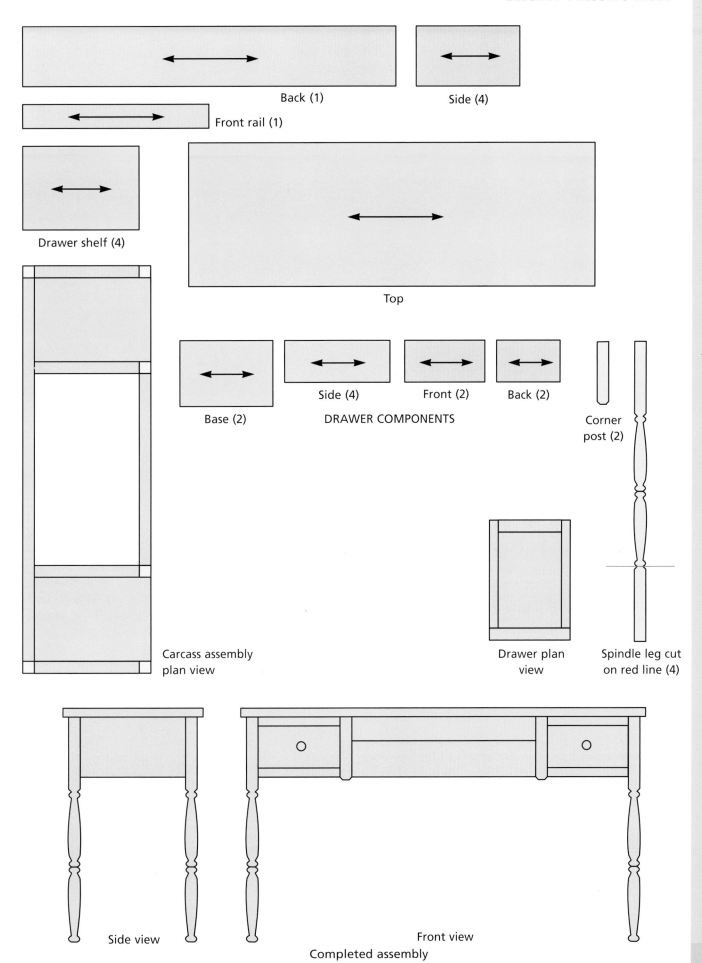

Back (1)

Side (4)

Front rail (1)

Drawer shelf (4)

Top

Base (2)

Side (4)

Front (2)

Back (2)

DRAWER COMPONENTS

Corner post (2)

Carcass assembly plan view

Drawer plan view

Spindle leg cut on red line (4)

Side view

Front view

Completed assembly

Dressing Stool

MATERIALS	TOOLS
Stair spindles	Ruler and pencil
Basswood (or other	Craft set
wood of your choice)	Abrasive
³⁄₁₆in and ⅛in thick	
Glue	
Sanding sealer	
Primer and paint/stain	
and varnish	
Fabric	
Synthetic wadding	

METHOD

1 Cut all components as shown on the drawing.

2 Assemble and glue together two end frames, using two legs and a side frame for each. The tops of the legs must be level with the top edge of the side frame, and the larger surfaces should be flush with the squared portion of the stair spindle legs, sanding flush if necessary.

3 Place the base on a flat smooth surface, then assemble and glue together the frame around this as shown in the plan view on the drawing. Make sure that all corners are square and that the legs and frame sections are truly vertical.

4 When this is dry, sand very lightly, remove all sanding dust and apply a coat of primer. Leave to dry thoroughly.

5 Sand very lightly with very fine grade abrasive, remove the sanding dust and apply the top coat.

6 After the top coat has dried, check the seat will fit in the top when there is fabric surrounding it, sanding the edges slightly until it just fits.

7 Cut a piece of fabric to the pattern given on the drawing. Add a small amount of synthetic wadding to the top of the seat. Place the fabric on a clean dry surface, with the WRONG side facing upwards. Invert the seat and wadding on the centre of this, and glue the edges of the fabric to the underside of the seat, keeping the edges, particularly the corners, as neat and smooth as possible.

8 Turn the now-padded seat the right way up and insert in the stool. Making it this way allows you to make replacement seats and have a change of seat as often as you like by cutting extra seats and using different fabrics.

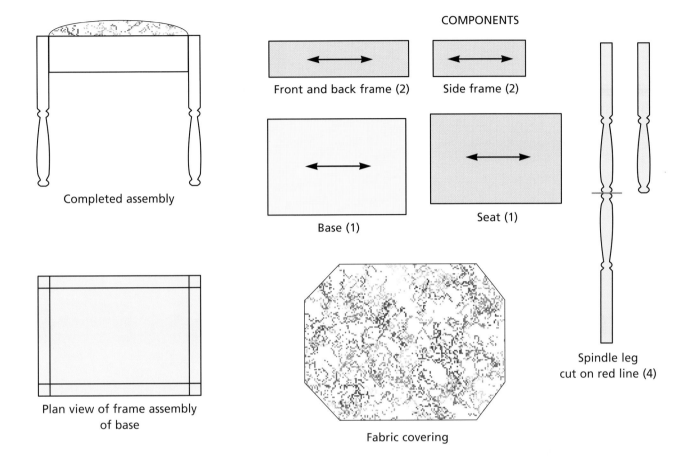

Completed assembly

COMPONENTS

Front and back frame (2)

Side frame (2)

Base (1)

Seat (1)

Plan view of frame assembly
of base

Fabric covering

Spindle leg
cut on red line (4)

Victorian Toilet Mirror

MATERIALS	TOOLS
Basswood ³⁄₃₂in thick, ⅛in thick and ¹⁄₁₆in thick	Craft set
Stair spindles	Razor saw
Mirror sheet	Drill and drill bit
Brass pins	
Small brass knobs	
Sanding sealer	
Finish of your choice	

METHOD

1   Cut the components for the carcass and drawer as shown on the drawing. The mirror back, mirror material and spacers can be cut either now or later. The frame pieces (coloured turquoise) are best cut to size later.

2   Make the holes in the two mirror supports for the pivot pin, then assemble and glue together the back and the two mirror supports. The bottom of the mirror supports and the bottom edge of the back must be level, and the faces of the mirror supports and back must be flush. Sand if necessary.

3   Place the drawer base on a smooth flat surface, then assemble the drawer around this and glue together. Make sure that it is perfectly square and that the vertical bits are truly vertical.

Tip: A piece of cling film tightly and smoothly covering the support surface will help to prevent the surface gluing itself to the drawer parts.

4   Drill two tiny holes in the drawer front for the knobs, but don't fix the knobs yet. Insert two large-headed pins through these holes from the INSIDE as a temporary aid in getting the drawer in and out as the assembly progresses.

Tip: Use the drawer, tightly encased in cling film, as a guide to the spacing when assembling the rest of the carcass.

5   Assemble and glue together the already assembled back and mirror supports, the bottom, sides and top. A cross-section view is shown on the drawing

6   Finally, add the upper top, making sure that the edges of it line up with the bottom. This completes the carcass and drawer.

7   If you haven't already done so, cut the pieces for the mirror now. This part is quite simple, except that you need to be able to paint the mirror back and surround without getting paint on the mirror material. For this reason, leave the bottom spacer loose, to be fitted later. Glue the two long side spacers and the top spacer to the mirror back, keeping the edges flush. When this is dry, the frame can be glued over the top. Use the bottom spacer to get the gap right, but don't let it get glued in place. Remove the bottom spacer again and you should be able to slip the mirror material in place temporarily – just to check that all is well and it will fit properly. Remove it again and set aside with the bottom spacer to be added when the painting is done and is dry.

8   Decide on the finish you want, and apply it to the assembled parts. The Victorians were very fond of ebonised furniture (that is, furniture made to look like ebony – black, with a satin finish). They were also addicted to japanned furniture, the English version of the oriental lacquered furniture: gloss black with gold decoration would give this effect. Alternatively, if you make the Elegant Dressing Table (see p. 104), this piece could be given the same finish and used in combination with it as shown in the drawing.

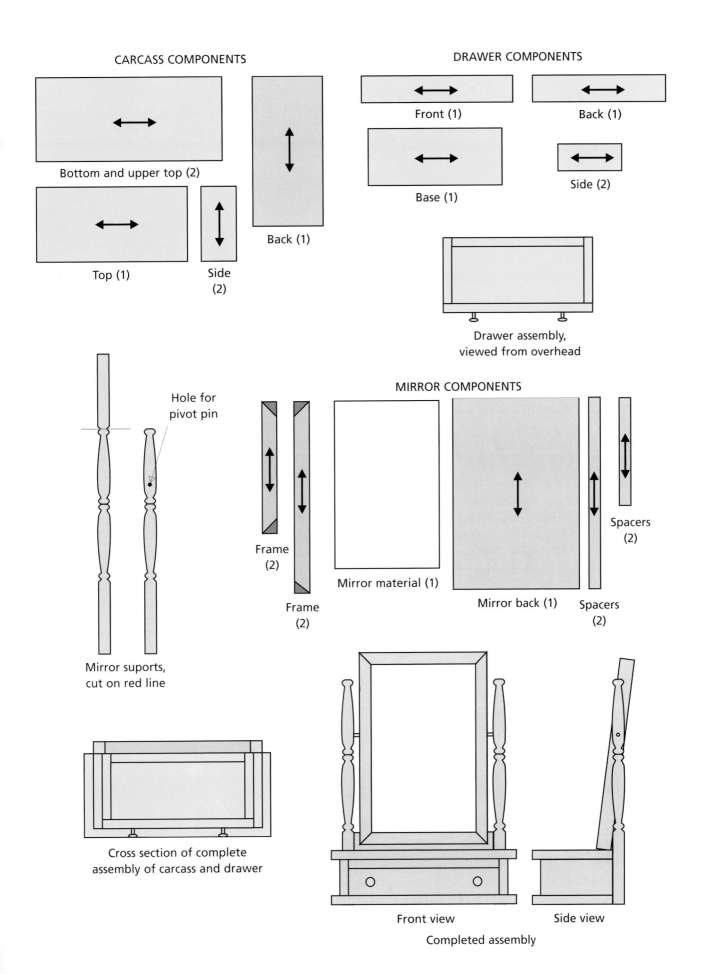

CARCASS COMPONENTS

Bottom and upper top (2)

Top (1)

Side (2)

Back (1)

DRAWER COMPONENTS

Front (1)

Back (1)

Base (1)

Side (2)

Drawer assembly,
viewed from overhead

Hole for
pivot pin

MIRROR COMPONENTS

Frame (2)

Frame (2)

Mirror material (1)

Mirror back (1)

Spacers (2)

Spacers (2)

Mirror suports,
cut on red line

Cross section of complete
assembly of carcass and drawer

Front view

Side view

Completed assembly

Stick Back Kitchen Chair with Turned Legs

MATERIALS

Lime or basswood

¾₁₆in thick

Turned parts as shown

Sanding sealer

Stain and varnish,

or acrylic paint

TOOLS

Ruler and pencil

Craft set

Drill and drill bits

METHOD

Remember that if you want a stained finish, the stain must go on before the glue.

1   Cut the blanks for the seat and top of back from the drawing and mark in the diagonals on one side, which will be the underneath of the seat.

2   The top of the back needs shaping. Drawing (a) shows the corners rounded off and the ends tapered slightly. Also shown is a cross-section with the ends also rounded. Either cut or sand the seat to shape: see (b) on the drawing.

3   Drill shallow holes (don't go right through) to accept the legs. They need to be centred over the diagonals that you marked earlier, as shown in drawing (c).

4   Next come the holes for the back posts and back sticks. The positioning for these is clearly shown on the drawings. Drawing (d) shows the ones in the top surface of the seat, and drawing (e) shows the corresponding holes in the underneath surface of the top of the back. Again, don't go right through.

Tip: A photocopy temporarily attached to the surface may help you to get these right.

5   Next come the holes in the legs for the stretchers. The positions can be seen on the completed assembly drawings. Mark all around each leg ¾₁₆in from the bottom: this will give you the heights, and help to get the stretchers level. You will also need a hole in the centre of each of two of the stretchers to take the centre one. Make sure that none of these holes goes right through.

6   Assemble the legs and stretchers to the seat first. Drawing (f) shows you what it should look like from underneath, which is probably the view you will have – it is easiest to place the seat on a flat surface with the underneath side facing upwards, gluing the legs to this, with the stretchers glued between them. Check that the chair stands level, and that the legs splay evenly before the glue finally sets though.

7   It is now relatively simple to assemble the back posts and back sticks to the chair seat, in the holes already made, with the top of the back and the corresponding holes holding the other ends of them.

8   A final light sanding (and then removing all dust) should give a good surface for the finish of your choice. Just varnish or wax for a natural look – or even paint your chair to match the kitchen.

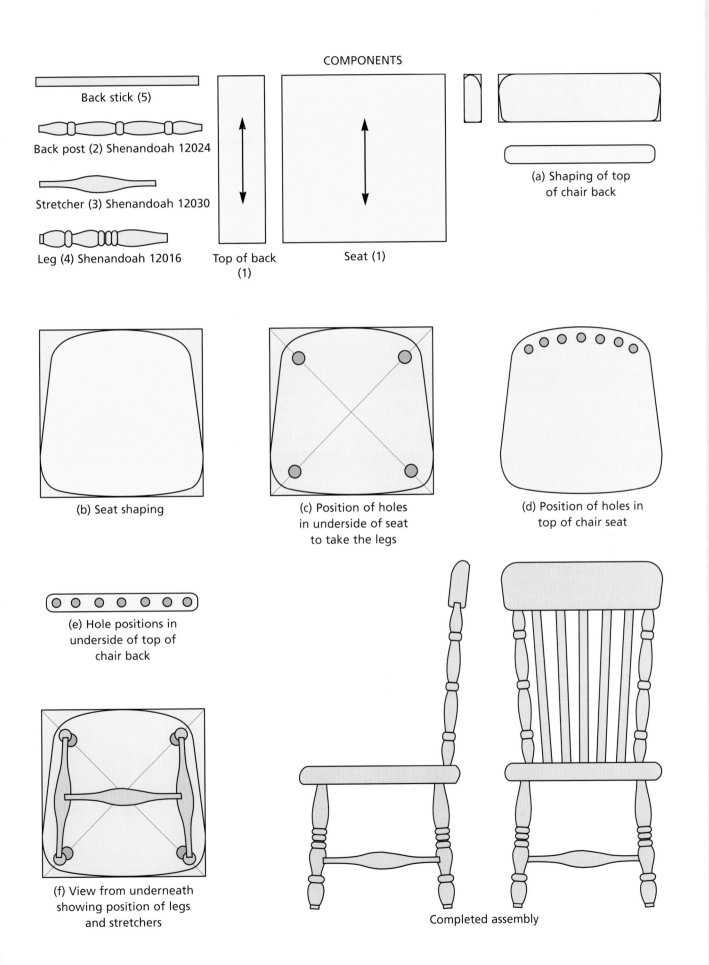

COMPONENTS

Back stick (5)

Back post (2) Shenandoah 12024

Stretcher (3) Shenandoah 12030

Leg (4) Shenandoah 12016

Top of back (1)

Seat (1)

(a) Shaping of top of chair back

(b) Seat shaping

(c) Position of holes in underside of seat to take the legs

(d) Position of holes in top of chair seat

(e) Hole positions in underside of top of chair back

(f) View from underneath showing position of legs and stretchers

Completed assembly

Another Stick Back Chair

MATERIALS

Lime or basswood
³⁄₁₆in thick
Turned parts
Sanding sealer
Stain and varnish,
or acrylic paint

TOOLS

Ruler and pencil
Craft set
Drill and drill bits

METHOD

Remember that if you want a stained finish, the stain must go on before the glue.

1   Cut the blanks for the seat and top of back from the drawing or cutting list, and mark in the diagonals on one side: this will be the underneath of the seat.

2   Either cut or sand the seat to shape: see (a) on the drawing. The top of the back also needs shaping, this time in two directions. Drawing (b) shows the top corners rounded off, and a cross section of the curve sanded on the two wider faces.

3   Drill shallow holes (don't go right through) to accept the legs. They need to be centred over the diagonals you marked earlier, as shown in drawing (c).

4   Next come the holes for the back posts and back sticks. The positioning for these is clearly shown on the drawings. Drawing (d) shows the ones in the top surface of the seat, and drawing (e) shows the corresponding holes in the underneath surface of the top of the back. Again, don't go right through.

5   Next come the holes in the legs for the stretchers (it's all holes, this bit!). The positions can be seen on the completed assembly drawings, the back and front ones being higher than the side ones, so that they don't interfere with one another. Mark all around each leg ⅞in from the bottom and 1¹⁄₁₆in from the bottom. This will give you the heights and will help to get the stretchers level. Don't forget that you will need to take care which side of the leg the holes are on, so that the relevant pairs of holes are opposite each other and not on the outside of the legs.

Tip: Drill the holes for one stretcher (say the front one), on each of two legs. Use a spare bit of cocktail stick just pushed in temporarily to join these together while you mark and drill the holes lower down for the side stretchers. This will also help to get the holes on the right part of the leg, and it will also stop the leg moving around while you make the new holes.

6   It is now simply a matter of gluing all the bits together. Assemble the legs and stretchers to the seat first. Drawing (f) shows you what it should look like from underneath – which is probably the view you will have. It is easiest to place the seat on a flat surface with the underneath side facing upwards, gluing the legs to this, with the stretchers glued between them. Do make sure that the chair stands level, and that the legs splay evenly before the glue finally sets though.

7   It is now relatively simple to assemble the back posts and back sticks to the chair seat, in the holes already made, with the top of the back and the corresponding holes holding the other ends of them.

8   A final light sanding should give a good surface for the finish of your choice. Just varnish or wax for a natural look, or paint the chair to match the kitchen. Remember to clean off all sanding dust.

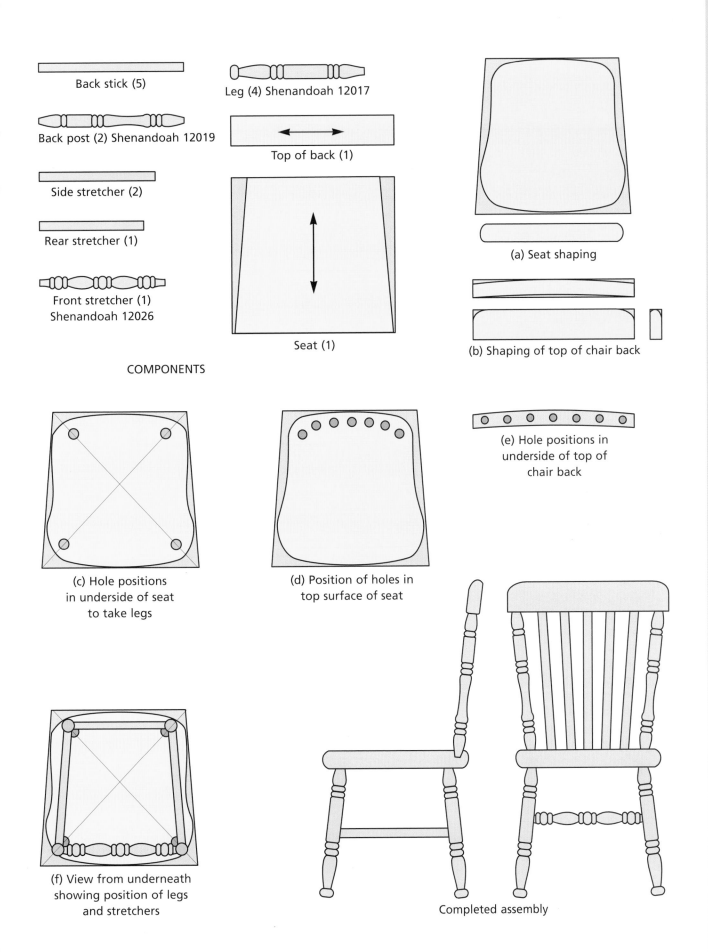

Back stick (5)

Leg (4) Shenandoah 12017

Top of back (1)

Back post (2) Shenandoah 12019

Side stretcher (2)

Rear stretcher (1)

Front stretcher (1)
Shenandoah 12026

Seat (1)

COMPONENTS

(a) Seat shaping

(b) Shaping of top of chair back

(c) Hole positions
in underside of seat
to take legs

(d) Position of holes in
top surface of seat

(e) Hole positions in
underside of top of
chair back

(f) View from underneath
showing position of legs
and stretchers

Completed assembly

Carving Chair

MATERIALS	TOOLS
Lime or basswood	Ruler and pencil
³⁄₁₆in thick	Craft set
Turned parts as shown	Drill and drill bits
Sanding sealer	
Stain and varnish	
or acrylic paint	

The carver is simply a stick back chair with arms, and is made in much the same way.

METHOD

Remember that if you want a stained finish, the stain must go on before the glue.

1 Cut the blanks for the seat and top of back from the drawing and mark in the diagonals on one side, which will be the underneath of the seat. Shape the seat as shown in drawing (a).

2 The top of the back needs shaping. Drawing (b) shows the corners rounded off and the ends shaped. Also shown is a cross section with the top edge rounded.

3 The arm rest should be shaped as shown in drawing (c).

4 Drill shallow holes (don't go right through) to accept the legs. They need to be centred over the diagonals you marked earlier, as shown in drawing (d)

5 Next come the holes for the back posts, back sticks and arm supports on the upper surface of the chair seat, and also for the back posts and back sticks on the underneath of the top of the chair back. The positioning for these is clearly shown on the drawings. Drawing (e) shows the ones in the top surface of the seat, and drawing (f) shows the corresponding holes in the underneath surface of the top of the back. Holes are also needed to take the top of the arm supports – drawing (c2) in the underneath surface of the arms. Again, don't go right through with any of these holes.

6 Now for the holes in the legs for the stretchers. The positions can be seen on the completed assembly drawings. Mark all around each leg to give you the heights and help to get the stretchers level. You will also need a hole in the centre of each of two of the stretchers to take the centre one. The back posts will each need a hole to accept the spigot on the end of the arm support. Mark this from the completed assembly (side view) drawing. Make sure that none of these holes goes right through.

7 Assemble the legs and stretchers to the seat first. Drawing (h) shows you what it should look like from undrneath, which is probably the view you will have, as it is easiest to place the seat on a flat surface with the underneath side facing upwards. Glue the legs to this with the strechers glued between them. Check, however, that the chair stands level, and that the legs splay evenly, before the glue finally sets.

8 It is now relatively simple to assemble the back posts and back sticks to the chair seat, in the holes already made, with the top of the back and the corresponding holes holding the other ends of them. Make sure that the holes in the back posts face the front.

9 The spindles used as arm supports need to be cut to length – drawing (g). The arms can now be added. The arm support spindles should be glued into the seat and the holes in the underneath of the arms, with the spigot at the other end of the arms glued into the holes in the back support posts.

10 A final light sanding should give a good surface for the finish of your choice. Just varnish for a natural look – perhaps wax, or even paint to match the kitchen.

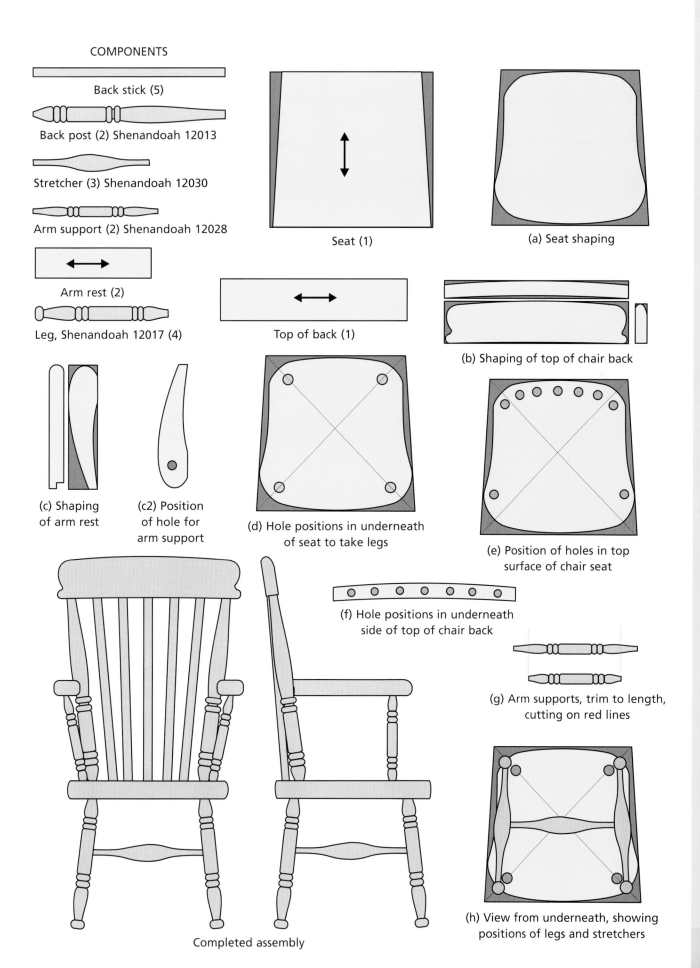

COMPONENTS

Back stick (5)

Back post (2) Shenandoah 12013

Stretcher (3) Shenandoah 12030

Arm support (2) Shenandoah 12028

Arm rest (2)

Leg, Shenandoah 12017 (4)

(c) Shaping of arm rest

(c2) Position of hole for arm support

Seat (1)

(a) Seat shaping

Top of back (1)

(b) Shaping of top of chair back

(d) Hole positions in underneath of seat to take legs

(e) Position of holes in top surface of chair seat

(f) Hole positions in underneath side of top of chair back

(g) Arm supports, trim to length, cutting on red lines

Completed assembly

(h) View from underneath, showing positions of legs and stretchers

Project miscellany

The items included here are somewhat more
complicated than those previously described. I begin
this section with two items actually made from pine,
showing how effective this can be if used with care –
and if you don't mind your equipment possibly
getting clogged with resin from this wood.

Pine Open Dresser

MATERIALS	TOOLS
Pine ⅛in thick	Craft set
Sanding sealer	Razor saw
Finish of your choice	Fret saw
Abrasive	(A mini table saw helps to make things quicker and more accurate)

METHOD

1 Cut all the components according to the drawing. If you don't have a fret saw, cut a rectangle for the trim, mark the fancy edge on this and sand to shape.

Tip: For sanding around curves, wrap a strip of abrasive around a piece of dowel or something similar.

2 Decide if you want to have the shaped bottom edge on the lower sides. Either cut this out with a fret saw and sand smooth, or remove as much as possible with a razor saw and then sand to shape.

3 Assemble the lower carcass first. Place the back on a flat smooth surface, then assemble and glue the other pieces to this. You will need the two sides to fit either side of the back, their top edges level with the top of the back. The lower top fits between the two sides and flush with the top of them. The bottom fits similarly, level with the bottom of the back, ⅜in up from the bottom edge of the sides.

4 The lower shelf also fits between the sides and up to the back. It must be glued in place absolutely level both from side to side and from front to back.

5 Finally, neaten the front and side edges of the potboard by sanding a small radius, and glue the potboard on top of the whole base carcass, keeping the back flush and overlapping the sides equally.

6 Now for the upper part again, work around the back on a flat smooth surface. Glue the sides and top in place. The top should be level with the top of each side, and flush with the top edge of the back.

7 Fix the shelves between the sides, tight up to the back. The spacing need not necessarily be the same as mine, as long as the shelves are level from side to side and back to front.

8 Place the lower assembly on its back on a smooth, flat surface. Check that the bottom of the upper assembly is completely smooth and level, sanding if necessary until it is. Place this on its back as well, and glue in place firmly to the top of the lower assembly.

9 To finish off the assembly, add the fancy trim strips. This makes a pleasing dresser as it is, but some pre-machined moulding cut to length and mitred at the corners really finishes the top off.

10 A clear finish is most effective with pine. Use either acrylic varnish or wax. Follow the usual finishing procedure of lightly sanding and removing all sanding dust before applying the finish. A coat of sanding sealer really helps on this resinous wood.

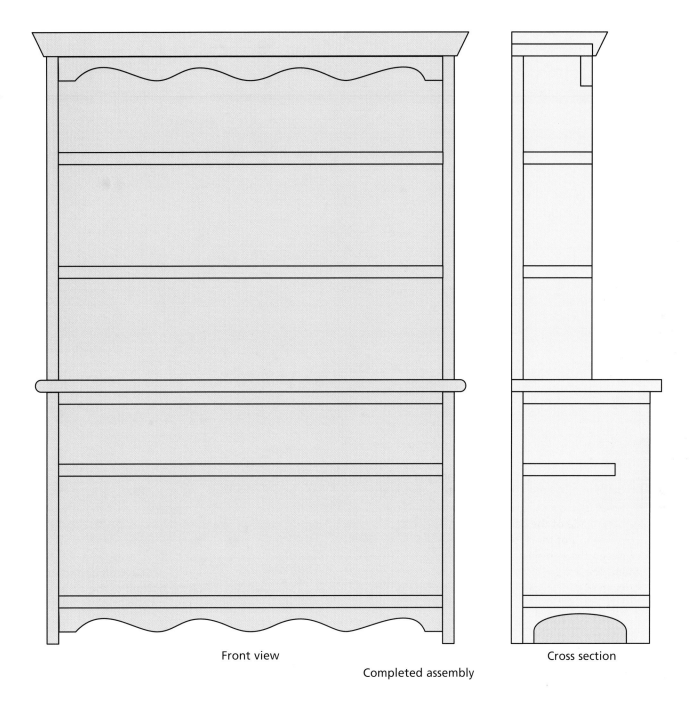

Front view

Completed assembly

Cross section

COMPONENTS

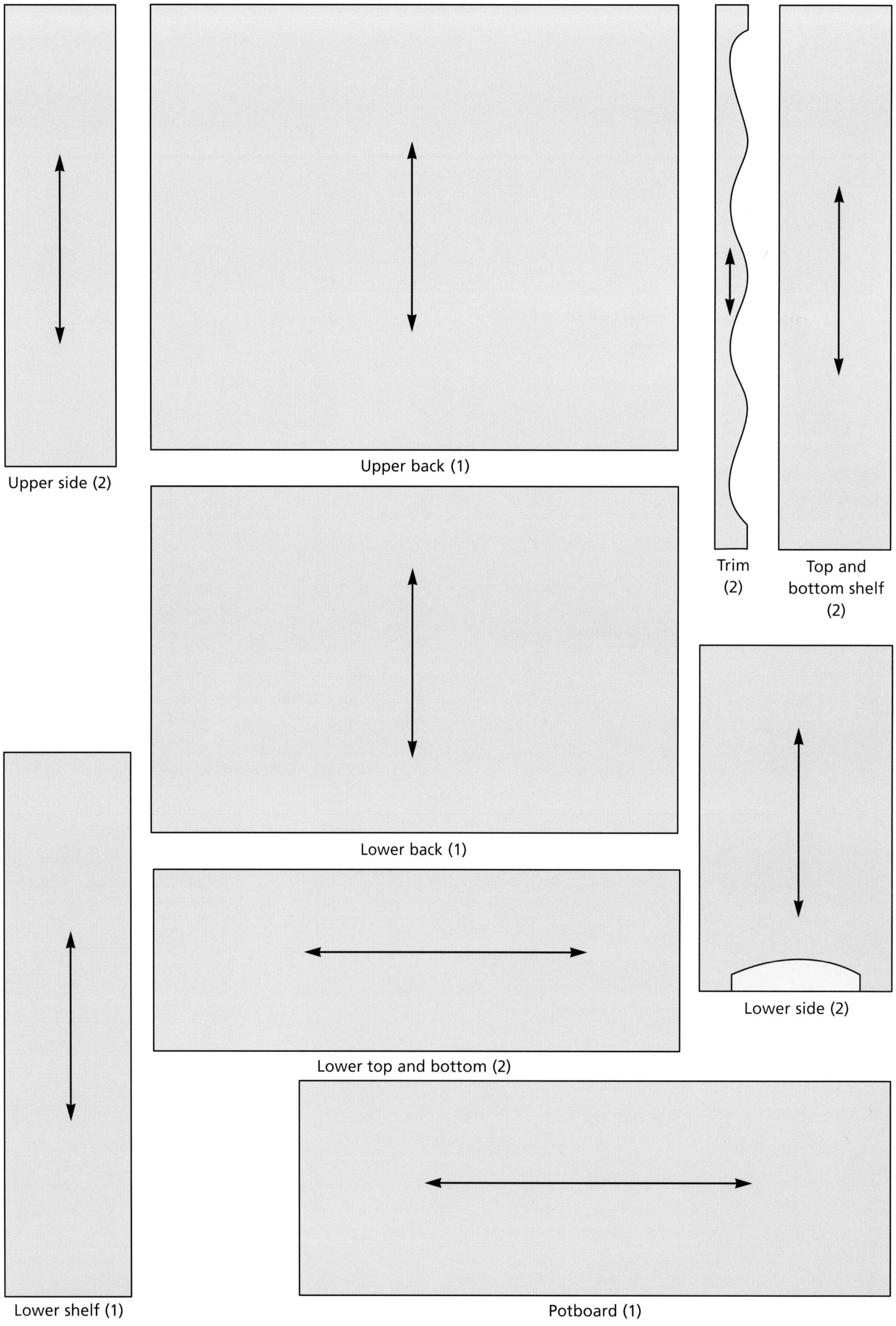

Upper side (2)

Upper back (1)

Trim (2)

Top and bottom shelf (2)

Lower back (1)

Lower side (2)

Lower top and bottom (2)

Lower shelf (1)

Potboard (1)

Pine Chest of Drawers

METHOD

1 Cut all the components from the drawing. Assemble and glue together the two sides of the carcass, using two legs and a side for each. The tops of the legs and the tops of the sides must be level and the sides flush with the legs to make two smooth units. Sand gently with the grain if necessary.

2 Assemble and glue together the main carcass box by placing the back on a flat, smooth surface, and then adding the two side assemblies and the top and bottom dust shelf dividers. The top must be level with the top of the back and the side assemblies, and the bottom in line with the bottom of the sides (not the bottom of the legs). Check everything is square, then clamp and leave for the glue to dry.

3 Make up each of the four drawers in a similar way around a drawer base, making sure that all is square (see drawer assembly plan view on drawing).

4 When the drawers are dry, check that they fit snugly between the sides of the main carcass. They should slip comfortably but not sloppily, and move in and out nicely on the bottom dust shelf divider. Sand carefully, little by little, and keep testing until they all do. Also check that all the drawers have a smooth bottom, or they will not work well.

5 Mark the positions for the knobs on the horizontal centre line and an equal distance from each side of each drawer front. Drill tiny holes.

Tip: Large-headed pins inserted temporarily in the knob holes from the INSIDE will help you to be able to get the drawers out until the knobs are fitted. There is nothing more frustrating than pushing a drawer into place and then not being able to get it out again – whether in miniature or full-size.

6 Have a trial assembly with no glue, to see that the drawers and intervening dust shelf dividers actually fit into the allotted space. If they don't, sand the drawers gently, bit by bit, until they do.

7 Cover the drawers tightly in smooth cling film to help prevent the glue sticking them in place, and use them as spacers to set the positions for the dust shelf dividers as they are glued in place.

8 The top can finally be glued on, centred carefully, and clamped down until dry.

9 Apply a coat of sanding sealer and give everything a final light sanding. Carefully remove every last vestige of sanding dust before applying the final coat of clear varnish to let the wood really show up.

CARCASS COMPONENTS

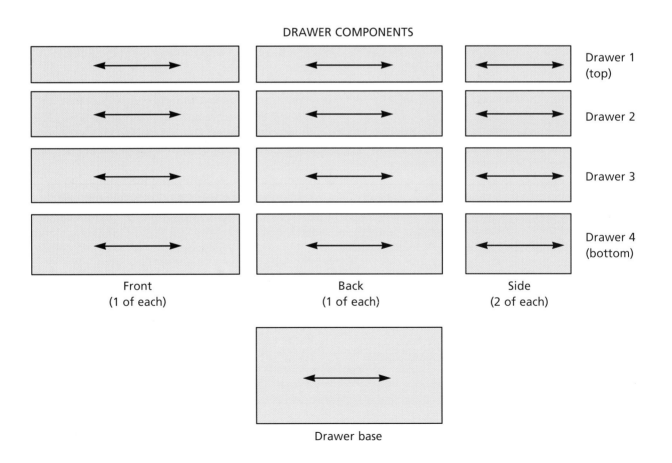

Back (4)

Side (2)

Top (1)

Drawer
shelf/divider (5)

Leg (4)

DRAWER COMPONENTS

Drawer 1
(top)

Drawer 2

Drawer 3

Drawer 4
(bottom)

Front
(1 of each)

Back
(1 of each)

Side
(2 of each)

Drawer base

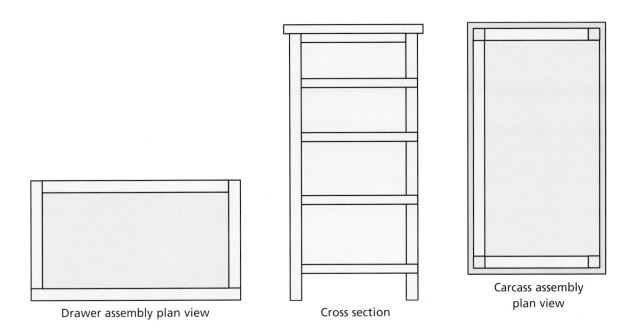

Drawer assembly plan view

Cross section

Carcass assembly
plan view

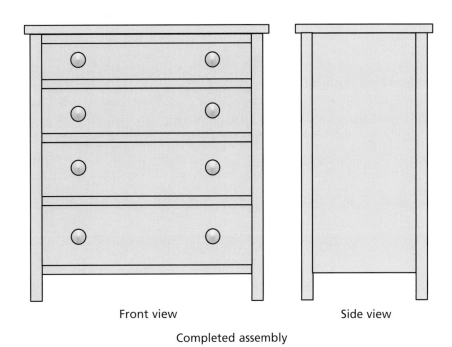

Front view

Side view

Completed assembly

Shop Fitting

Just for a change, I thought it would be nice to have a piece which could be used in a shop. As you will see, there are suggestions as to how it could be used in other settings with only minor modifications.

This design was originally made for a shop fitting, as shown here. The same basic design, perhaps made with pine, would make a very nice large dresser, particularly if doors were added to the lower section. Indeed, the lower section alone makes a good sideboard if given doors. If mahogany or walnut stripwood were used, and additional shelves added to the lower section, this could serve as a large bookcase. No doubt you will come up with any number of alternatives.

MATERIALS	TOOLS
⅟₁₆in thick ply	Craft knife
⅛in thick Obeche	Razor saw
Trim moulding	Mitre box
(Borcraft PF6 used)	Power table saw
	Power router
	Straight router bit

METHOD

1 Cut all the components as shown on the drawing.

2 The assembly is much the same as the Pine Dresser (p. 118), the main differences being the size of the bits and the fact that the lower carcass has vertical division – positioned as shown on the drawing – instead of a shelf.

Mine was finished with a dark stain varnish, to simulate the somewhat dingy looking Victorian-style shop fittings still around when I was a child.

Completed assembly front view

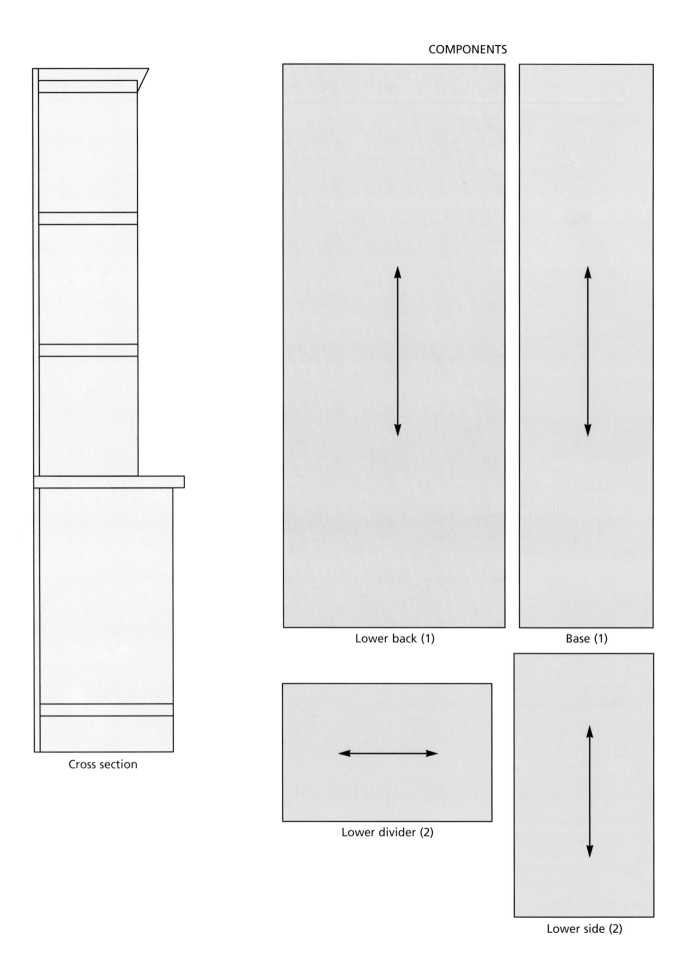

COMPONENTS

Lower back (1)

Base (1)

Cross section

Lower divider (2)

Lower side (2)

COMPONENTS

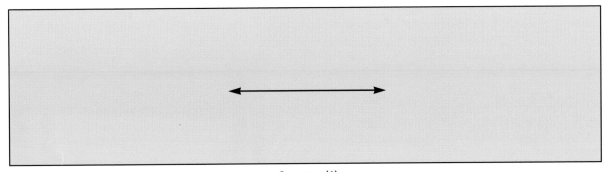

Counter (1)

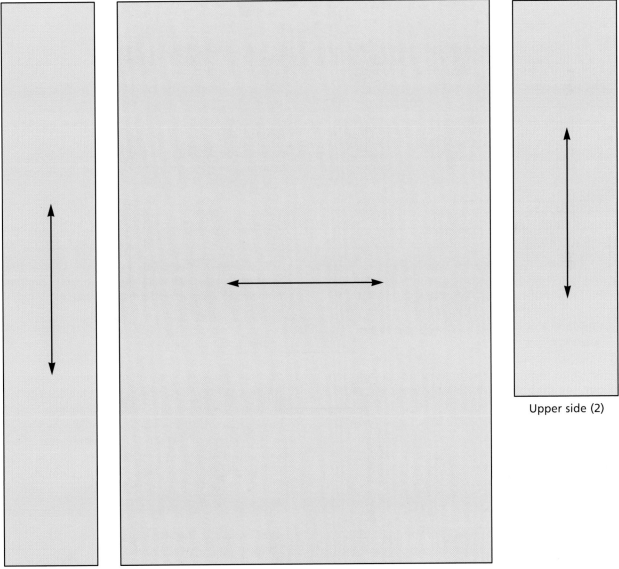

Upper shelf
and top (3)

Upper back (1)

Upper side (2)

Walnut Writing Desk or Side Table

MATERIALS

Walnut strip wood

1/16in, 3/32in, 1/8in, 3/16in thick

Wood glue

Finish of your choice

Pulls or knobs

TOOLS

Craft set

(A miniature bench type power saw could greatly help the accuracy)

METHOD

1   Cut out the number of components according to the size of the cutting templates shown in the drawings for framework and top components and for the drawer components. Make sure that the grain of the wood is running in the right direction. (See arrows.)

2   Sand all surfaces lightly, and do a 'dry run' assembly without glue to test that all parts fit well, making any slight adjustments that may be necessary before starting the final assembly.

3   For a neater final result, the upper edges of the top can be rounded over before assembly. If you intend to stain the piece, stain before starting to glue, because glue can prevent stain from penetrating the wood and will then leave ugly light-coloured patches.

4   Assemble the two side sections, using two legs and one side frame for each. The top of the legs must be flush with the top edge of the side frame. Glue the two side sections and the back frame around the edges of one of the drawer shelf/top frame pieces, so that all top edges are flush and everything is square.

5   To make the drawers, glue a drawer back, two sides and a front around the edges of the drawer base as shown in the drawer assembly drawing (p. 130). Finally, add the decorative drawer front centrally to the front of each drawer. Again, these can have the edges slightly rounded for a neater finish. The same method is used for all three drawers.

6   Making the drawers at this stage is a help when it comes to aligning the dividers and the lower drawer shelf/front frame. The dividers can be added now, making sure that they are absolutely square, and then the drawer support shelf can be added. The dotted lines on the frame assembly drawing indicate the position of the dividers, and the drawer shelf should be flush with the bottom edges of the back and side frames. Use the drawers to check that the spacing is correct, but make sure that they don't get glued into the assembly.

7   The addition of drawer pulls or knobs will add the final finishing touch to the appearance of the desk, and can be a great help if fixed in place temporarily now to aid in handling the drawers.

Tip: Cover in cling film.

8   With the drawers removed, glue the completed frame assembly to the lower top. It is easiest to lay the top on a flat surface with the underside facing upwards and turn the frame assemble upside down on top of this. When the glue has dried, turn the assembly the right way up again and add the upper top, positioning it centrally. A weight carefully placed on top of this will help to prevent distortion as the glue dries.

9   Apply whatever final finish you choose to use, following the manufacturers' instructions.

For a writing desk the upper top could have simulated leather material added in the centre, preferably inset slightly – if you are really ambitious.

FRAMEWORK and TOP COMPONENTS

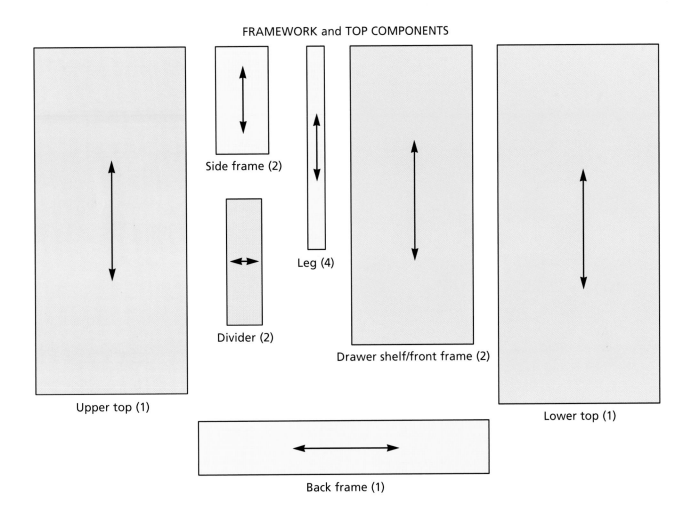

Upper top (1)

Side frame (2)

Divider (2)

Leg (4)

Drawer shelf/front frame (2)

Lower top (1)

Back frame (1)

DRAWER COMPONENTS

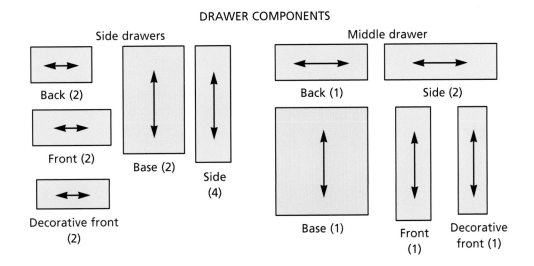

Side drawers

Back (2)

Front (2)

Decorative front (2)

Base (2)

Side (4)

Middle drawer

Back (1)

Side (2)

Base (1)

Front (1)

Decorative front (1)

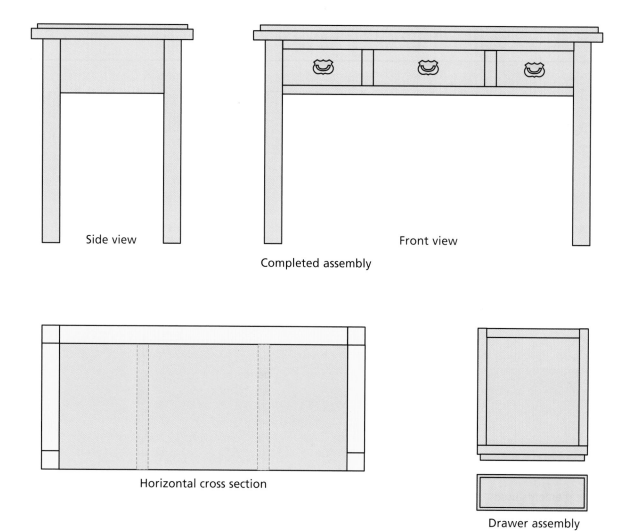

Side view

Front view

Completed assembly

Horizontal cross section

Drawer assembly

Portuguese-style Painted Furniture

On a visit to our Portuguese friends in the Algarve, I was interested to see their newly converted tourist accommodation. The buildings were originally farm buildings which have retained as much as possible of the original character. I was further delighted to see the furniture in some of the rooms. This was reproduction furniture made and decorated in typical Alentejo style. It is this furniture that forms the basis of the pieces included here.

Design elements and painting details

The originals had their designs painted by hand, so I thought it would be nice to try to do mine that way, too. If you would like to have a go yourself I have tried to give as much information as I can about how I paint mine. At first sight the painting looks somewhat daunting and complicated, but when you look more carefully, it can be broken down into units which are quite simple. Most of the design is made up of circles, or approximate circles, and dots. The colours used are actually very few: blue, red, yellow and white, plus green to save mixing the blue and yellow. The seemingly complicated shading on the larger floral motifs is done by adding a dab of white on the still-wet red or blue, giving it a slight swirl to mix with the colour beneath in a somewhat random way. Try it out on a spare bit of card: it isn't as bad as it looks, is it?

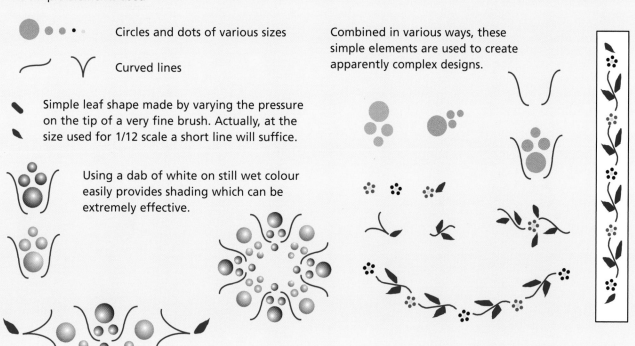

The simple elements used

Circles and dots of various sizes

Curved lines

Simple leaf shape made by varying the pressure on the tip of a very fine brush. Actually, at the size used for 1/12 scale a short line will suffice.

Using a dab of white on still wet colour easily provides shading which can be extremely effective.

Combined in various ways, these simple elements are used to create apparently complex designs.

Round Table

MATERIALS	TOOLS
Basswood (or similar)	Razor saw
⅛in and ¼in thick and	Mitre box
³⁄₁₆in square	Fretsaw
Sanding sealer	Abrasive
Paint	Clamps
Glue	

METHOD

1 Cut all components from the relevant material as shown on the drawing. For the lower top and shelf, first cut a rectangle, then remove a ³⁄₁₆in x ³⁄₁₆in square from each corner (see drawing). This needs to be done as accurately as possible so that the legs will fit well. This is necessary to hold everything together firmly and squarely.

2 Assemble the lower top. shelf and the four legs, (see assembly drawing). The shelf should be exactly the same distance from the bottom of each leg as shown, and the tops of all four legs must be flush with the top surface of the lower top. Clamp together, check everything is completely square and leave for the glue to dry.

3 Glue the assembly to the top, making sure that it is exactly centred. It is easier to do this with the top on the working surface, then you can see what you are doing when the assembly is turned upside down and glued to it.

4 Sand lightly, remove all traces of sanding dust and apply a coat of sanding sealer. When the sealer is dry, sand again and remove all sanding dust.

5 Paint in the colour of your choice. Then, when this is completely dry, either hand paint the suggested design onto the table, or apply transfers according to the manufacturers' instructions.

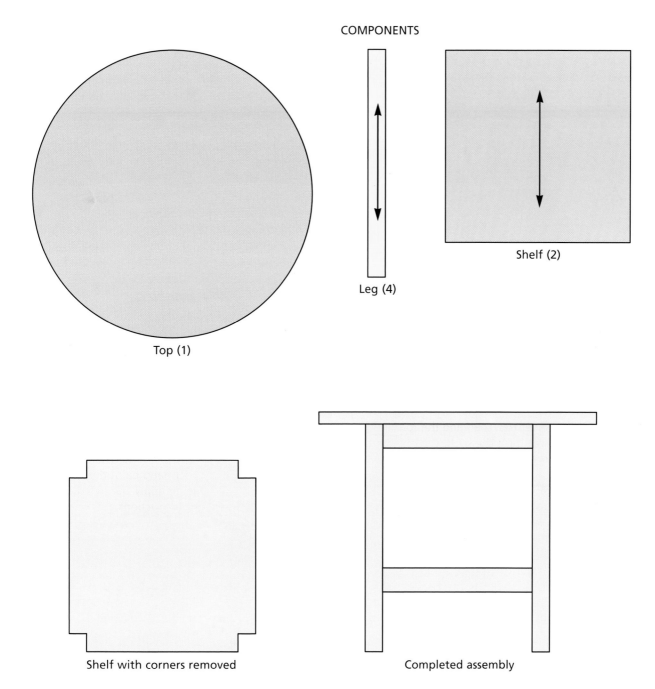

COMPONENTS

Top (1)

Leg (4)

Shelf (2)

Shelf with corners removed

Completed assembly

Painting a Round Table

To enable you to copy my version of the Portuguese style of painting, I have included some fairly detailed drawings.

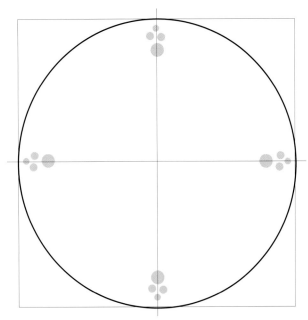

Draw a circle, radius 1⅛in to represent the table top, then draw two lines through the centre of the circle and at right angles to each other. The first four groups of flowers in the outer circle are positioned on these.

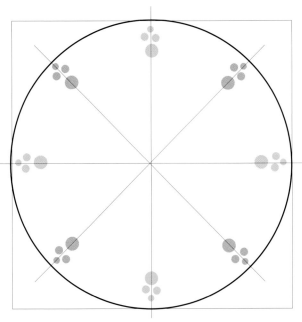

The remaining four main groups in the outer circle are positioned midway between these.

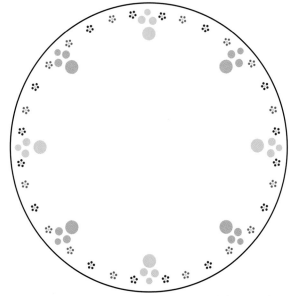

Small daisies made up of five coloured dots with a yellow dot in the centre are spaced at approximately equal intervals between the main flower groups.

Link the daisies together with a fine green line and two simple leaves (or small lines, see page 131) and finally add two curved lines as leaves for each main flower group.

This makes an attractive design on its own. To work the full design add inner circles of flower groups, daisies, green lines and leaves in a similar way. Refer to the full design (shown opposite) for the relative positions.

Full design shown actual size.
The whole of the design does not need to be used
to create an attractive table top.
A few alternatives are shown here.

To keep the middle of the table clear
omit the centre of the design.

Using just the centre and outer circle of the design
creates a table top with a more open design.

A pretty example using only the simple daisy flower
motifs of the outer edge and the middle of the design.

Single Bed

METHOD

1 Cut components to size, as shown on the full size drawing. If you don't have a fretsaw for the curved cut-outs on the head and foot boards, the following method will work. Measure ⅝in from the top corners across the top towards the centre and down each side. Join these two points and cut on this line. Then mark the curve and sand down to the marked line.

2 Assemble together each of the bed ends, with the headboard between the two head posts and the footboard between the two foot posts. Make sure that they are square, an equal distance from the bottom of the posts, and in the centre of the width of the posts.

3 Glue a support strip at the bottom of each of the head and foot boards: this will carry the mattress support later.

4 Glue on the ornament at the top of the bed posts. If you are using a wooden door knob or turned finial, drill a small hole for the spigot and glue the ornament in this for a firm fixing. Now add the trim strips to the centre of each bed end – the shorter one first, then the bigger one on top. They should be centred neatly over one another with equal overlaps on both sides (see assembly drawing opposite).

5 Assemble and glue together the mattress support and the two side rails as shown on the drawing.

6 Coat all the pieces with sanding sealer. Sand lightly when dry, then apply a primer coat and sand again when dry. Remove all traces of sanding dust carefully.

7 Apply the top coat and allow to dry thoroughly before attempting any decoration. A suggested design is shown to size. If you don't fancy hand-painting your design, there are many small transfers available from specialist suppliers.

8 For a permanent assembly, glue the already assembled mattress support and side rails on top of the support strips of the head and foot boards. If you want to be able to take the item apart, drill two small holes at each end through the mattress support and the support strip, and insert two small screws or pins.

9 A piece of foam or balsa about ⅛in shorter than the mattress support can be covered neatly with cotton material and placed on top of the mattress support. Add a pillow and some bedclothes for a really pretty finish.

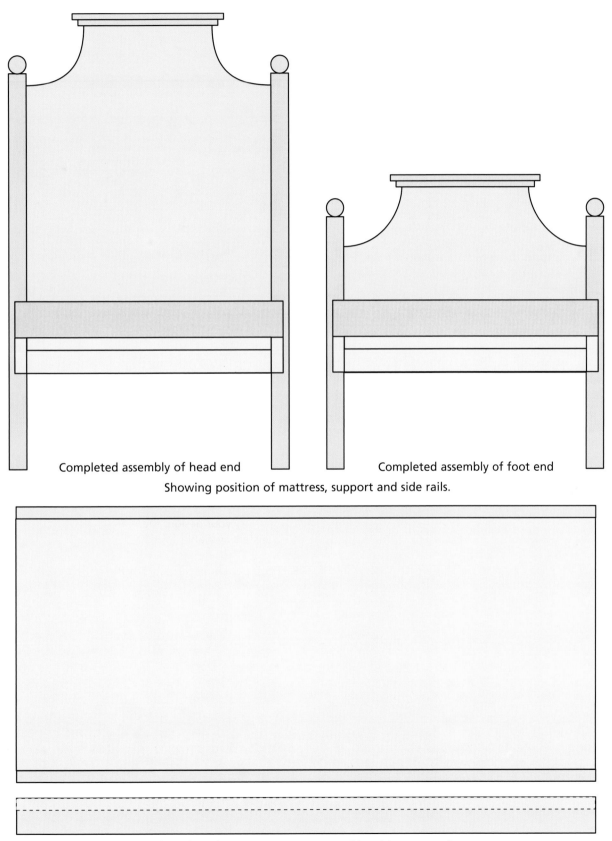

Completed assembly of head end   Completed assembly of foot end

Showing position of mattress, support and side rails.

Side rails and mattress support assembly with cross section.
Dotted lines showing relative position of side rail and mattress support.

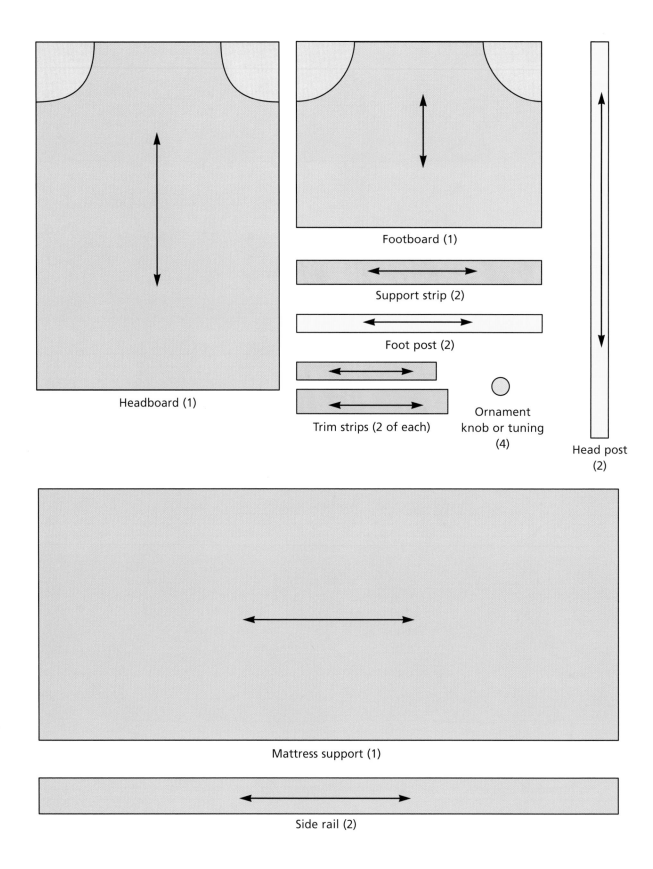

Headboard (1)

Footboard (1)

Support strip (2)

Foot post (2)

Trim strips (2 of each)

Ornament knob or tuning (4)

Head post (2)

Mattress support (1)

Side rail (2)

COMPONENTS

Decoration suggestion
Cross section of mattress and pillow show the positions in relation to the decoration.

Bedside Cabinet

MATERIALS	TOOLS
Model ply ¹⁄₁₆in thick	Ruler and pencil
Basswood (or similar)	Craft set
³⁄₁₆in square	Abrasive
Strip wood ⅛in thick	Bar clamps
and ³⁄₃₂in thick	
Primer	
Paint	
Glue	

METHOD

1 Cut all the components from the drawing. Assemble and glue together the two sides of the carcass, using two legs and a side for each. The tops of the legs and the tops of the sides must be level. There must be one flat side to each assembly, with the face of the side flush with the legs. (This is so that the drawers will not be obstructed.) Sand gently with the grain on this side when the glue is dry.

2 Assemble and glue together the main carcass box by placing the back on a flat smooth surface, then adding the two side assemblies and the top and bottom dust shelf dividers. The top must be level with the top of the back and the side assemblies, and the bottom one in line with the bottom of the sides. Check that everything is square, then clamp and leave for the glue to dry.

3 Make up each of the drawers with a front, back and two sides around a drawer base, making sure that all is square (see drawer assembly plan view on drawing). Leave the decorative fronts off for the moment, though.

4 When the drawers are dry, check that they fit snugly between the sides of the main carcass. They should slip comfortably, but not sloppily, and move in and out nicely on the bottom shelf. Sand carefully, little by little, and keep testing until they all do. Also check that both drawers have a smooth bottom, or they will not work well for long.

5 Mark the positions for the knobs on the horizontal centre line and an equal distance from each side of each drawer front. Drill tiny holes.

Tip: Large-headed pins inserted temporarily in the knob holes from the INSIDE will help you to be able to get the drawers in and out until the knobs are fitted.

6 Have a trial assembly with no glue, to see that the drawers and intervening shelf actually do fit into the allotted space. If not, sand the drawers gently, bit by bit until they do.

7 Cover the drawers tightly in smooth clingfilm to help prevent the glue sticking them in place, and use them as spacers to set the positions for the remaining shelf as it is glued in place.

8 Now the decorative drawer fronts can be glued on. Position them so that they look right when the drawers are closed. Careful adjustments at this stage can cover a multitude of sins if the drawers don't fit too well. When you are happy, glue them on and add the knobs.

9 The top can finally be glued on, centred carefully (see plan view of carcass) and clamped down until dry.

10 Apply a coat of sanding sealer and give everything a final light sanding. Carefully remove every last vestige of sanding dust before applying the final coat of paint.

11 All you have to do now is paint of the decorations. There are two suggested painting schemes shown. You could use tiny transfers, available from specialist stockists, if this seems too complicated.

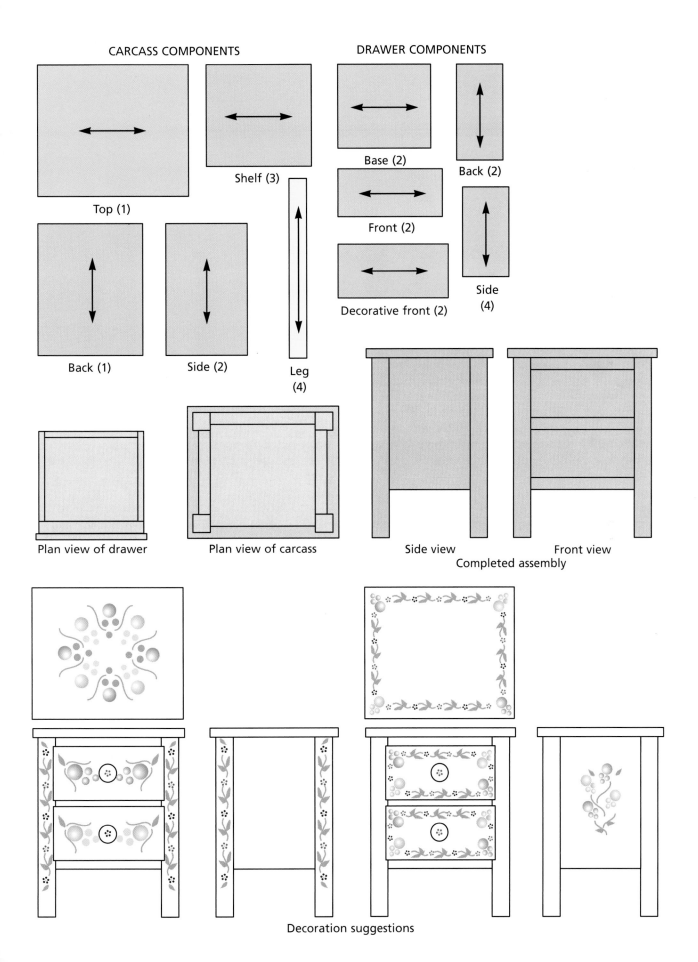

CARCASS COMPONENTS

Top (1)

Shelf (3)

Back (1)

Side (2)

Leg (4)

DRAWER COMPONENTS

Base (2)

Back (2)

Front (2)

Side (4)

Decorative front (2)

Plan view of drawer

Plan view of carcass

Side view

Front view

Completed assembly

Decoration suggestions

Armoire or Wardrobe

Ideally you need a small power table saw for cutting plywood. It can be done with a craft set but is much simpler and more accurate with a power saw.

METHOD

1   Cut all the components from the drawing. Assemble and glue together the two sides of the carcass using two legs and a side for each. The tops of the legs and the tops of the sides must be level. There must be one flat side to each assembly, with the face of the side flush with the legs. This is the inside face, and allows the drawer to fit and work easily. Sand gently with the grain on this side when the glue is dry.

2   Assemble and glue together the main carcass using the already assembled sides, joining them with the back, fitting flush with the top of the two sides and the back face of the back legs, and two of the shelves, one of which fits flush with the top of the sides and the other flush with the bottom edge of the back and absolutely level and square with the bottom edges of the two sides (see cross sectional drawing).

3   Assemble and glue together the drawer (see plan view (c)) with the front, back and sides around the base.

4   Make up the centre post (see plan view of carcass (b) and cross section drawing (a)) from ³⁄₁₆in square and a ⁵⁄₁₆in wide strip of ¹⁄₁₆in thick ply or strip wood centred on one face.

5   Assemble and glue together two identical doors (see door assembly drawing (d)), with the rails and stiles firmly and squarely glued to the face of the ⅛in ply.

6   Using the drawer and doors to check the spacing, insert and glue in position the remaining shelf and the centre post.

You will probably need to do a little careful sanding to get all these bits to fit together neatly. Just take time and sand only a little at a time, testing and trying then sanding again until the necessary fit is achieved.

7   Position and glue in place tiny hinges, add the knobs, and the construction is done. Now all you have to do is paint it! Follow the method given for the bedside cabinet. A suggested painting scheme is shown in the illustration on p. 146, although the photograph above is of the wardrobe before the decorative flower motifs were added. Compare this with the other items in this section and it just shows how much more attractive a few flowers make things look.

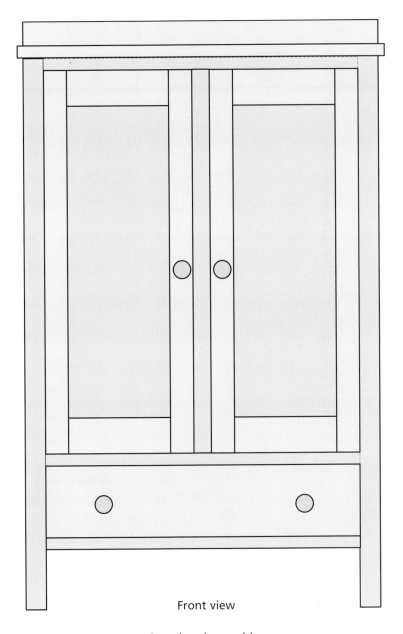

Front view

Completed assembly

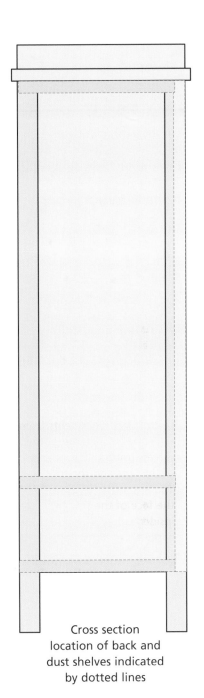

Cross section
location of back and
dust shelves indicated
by dotted lines

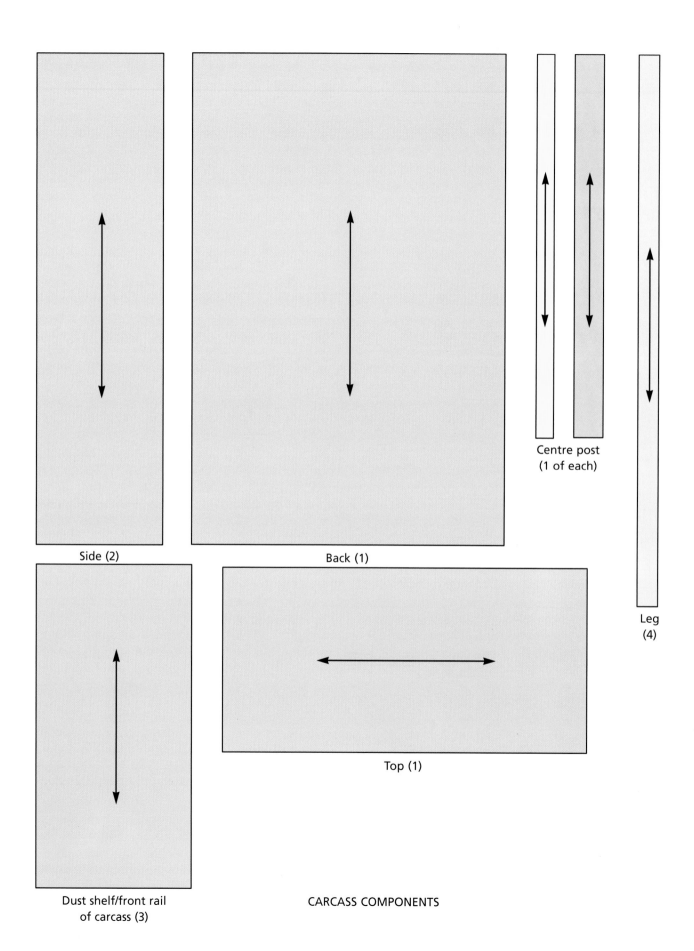

Side (2)

Back (1)

Centre post
(1 of each)

Leg
(4)

Dust shelf/front rail
of carcass (3)

Top (1)

CARCASS COMPONENTS

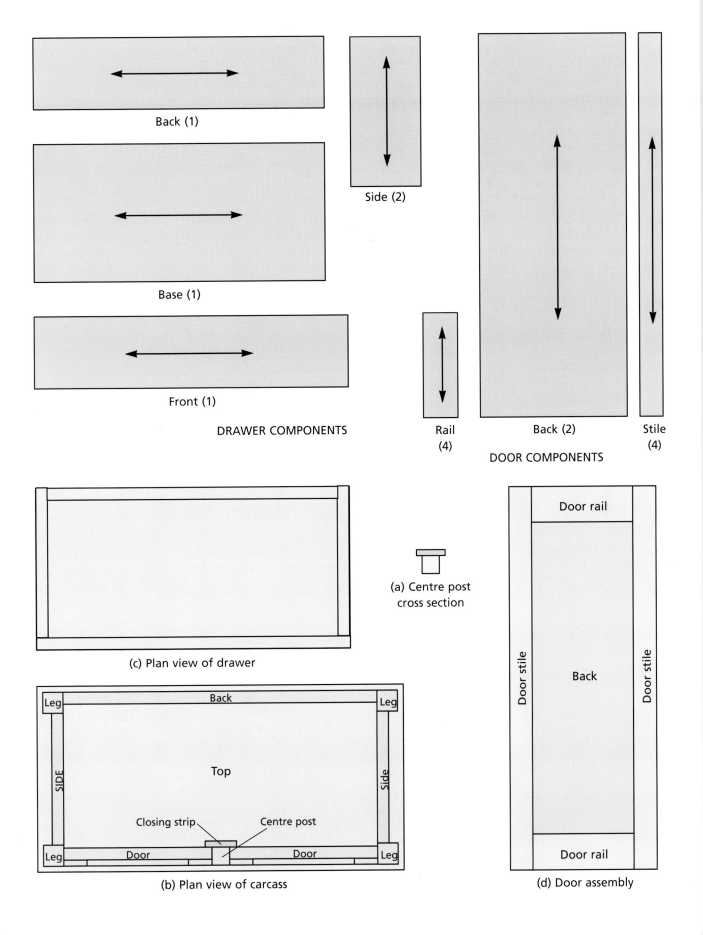

Back (1)

Base (1)

Front (1)

Side (2)

DRAWER COMPONENTS

Rail
(4)

Back (2)

Stile
(4)

DOOR COMPONENTS

(a) Centre post
cross section

(c) Plan view of drawer

Leg   Back   Leg

SIDE   Top   Side

Closing strip   Centre post

Leg   Door   Door   Leg

(b) Plan view of carcass

Door rail

Door stile   Back   Door stile

Door rail

(d) Door assembly

Front view with suggestion for decoration

Chair with Rush Seating

MATERIALS

Basswood (or similar)
³⁄₁₆in square and
³⁄₃₂in thick
Dowel ³⁄₃₂in diameter
(Cocktail sticks)
Primer
Paint
Glue
Raffia

TOOLS

Ruler and pencil
Craft set
Abrasive
Bar clamps

METHOD

1 Cut all the components from the drawing. For the shaped top rail either cut to shape with a fret saw, or cut the rectangle, transfer the curved shape and sand to shape.

2 Mark the positions and drill holes for the seat rails and stretchers, in a similar way as detailed for the stool frame on p. 77.

3 Assemble and glue together two side frames using one front leg, one back leg, a side rail and a dowel stretcher for each.

4 Joint the two side frames together with the top rail and lower rail of the back, and remaining seat rails and stretchers (see assembly drawings).

5 Sand lightly, remove all sanding dust and paint using a coat of primer first.

6 Use raffia to create the rush seating effect (see p. 79 for basic guidance). The one shown in the photograph has a slightly different arrangement by making two figure-of-eight turns between the side rails only across the front of the seat to give a deep seat effect. There will be space left on the front and back rails by the time the side rails are full, fill these by using figure-of-eight movements between the front and back rails.

7 Now add the painted flower detail. A suggested painting scheme is shown on p.148.

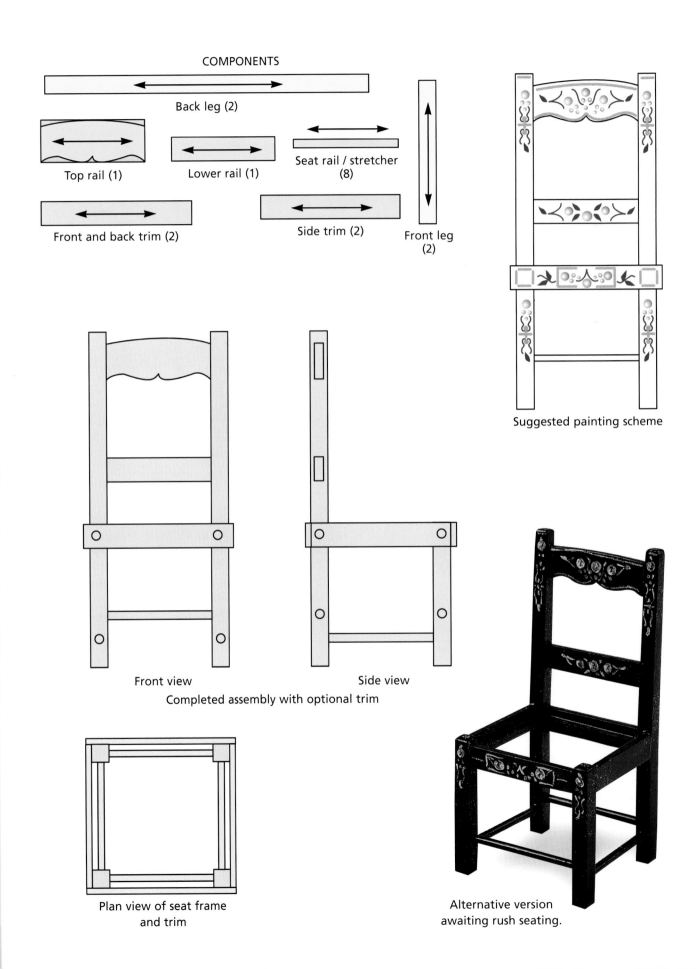

COMPONENTS

Back leg (2)

Top rail (1)

Lower rail (1)

Seat rail / stretcher (8)

Front and back trim (2)

Side trim (2)

Front leg (2)

Suggested painting scheme

Front view

Side view

Completed assembly with optional trim

Plan view of seat frame and trim

Alternative version awaiting rush seating.

Wall Mirror

MATERIALS	TOOLS
Basswood (or model ply) ⅟₁₆in, ³⁄₃₂in and ½in thick	Ruler and pencil
Ornament – part of pre-machined turned item or small bead.	Craft set
Mirror material	Abrasive
Primer and paint	Bar clamps
Glue	

METHOD

1 Cut all the components from the drawing. For the shaped top either cut to shape with a fret saw, or cut the blank, transfer the curved shape and sand to shape.

2 Assemble and glue together the frame, making sure that everything is square and that the front surface is flush before clamping and leaving to set.

3 Glue the trim strips in place on top of the centre portion of the top frame, and the ornaments on the top of the side frames.

Tip: A tiny hole and part of a small pin in the centre of the top of each side frame for a dowel will help to make the fastening of this more secure.

4 Sand really smooth, remove all traces of sanding dust and paint.

5 When the all-over paint is dry, add the flower motif decoration, then the mirror material can be positioned and held in place by either gluing the back over it or simply using adhesive tape which won't be seen on the back.

If you want hanging strings to show, fix to the back of the mirror before attaching to the wall, or simply fix the mirror straight onto the wall using something like Blu–Tak so that it can be removed when required.

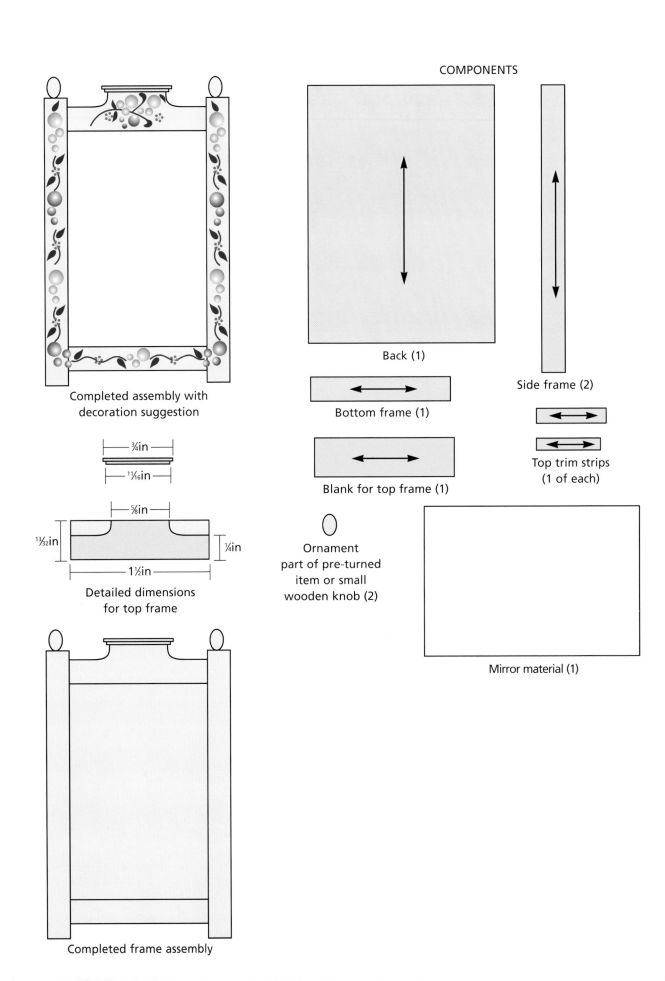

Completed assembly with
decoration suggestion

¾in

1¹¹⁄₁₆in

⅝in

13³⁄₃₂in   ¼in

1½in

Detailed dimensions
for top frame

Completed frame assembly

COMPONENTS

Back (1)

Side frame (2)

Bottom frame (1)

Blank for top frame (1)

Top trim strips
(1 of each)

Ornament
part of pre-turned
item or small
wooden knob (2)

Mirror material (1)

Trimmings & Needlework

To add the finishing touches, particularly to upholstered furniture, it is not always easy to find a suitable braid or trimming in the right colour or size. So here are a few examples of some which you can make for yourself. All the necessary instructions are shown on the relevant drawings.

Why not have a go at making some cushions or mats to enhance some of your furniture projects? Working charts and suggestions are included for Bargello and Portuguese style.

TRIMMINGS
Plait Braid

Perhaps the easiest way to make a braid to add to the edge of your upholstery is to plait threads of various kinds. Stranded embroidery thread, crochet thread or very fine knitting yarn can all be used, as indeed, for a much bolder effect, can very narrow ribbon.

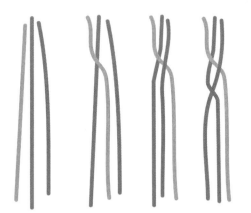

To create a braid repeat the sequence: left over right, right over left, until desired length has been worked.

Crochet Chain Braid

Crochet a chain of the required length using embroidery thread, crochet thread or any other thread of similar thickness which will look right with your piece of furniture. You will need thread and a crochet hook of a suitable size for your chosen thread. The one shown on the blanket box was worked with a 1.5mm hook and 20 crochet cotton. Different and interesting effects result from using two or three strands of finer thread in different colours.

If you want a fringe, here is one that can be stitched directly onto the edge of the fabric, either to finish off the upholstery, or to edge a mat or rug.

Simple looped or fringed edging

Can be used on mats, bed covers, curtains, cushions.

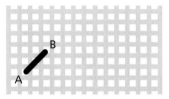

Start with needle through to front at A.
First stitch (shown black A-B).
Follow black line diagonally left to right, needle to back.

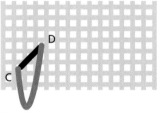

Needle to back again in same place as end of first stitch, leaving loose loop. Loop stitch (shown brown C-D). Needle to front again two threads immediately below D.

Last stitch (shown green E-F). Needle to back above where first stitch started (F). To start next set of stitches.

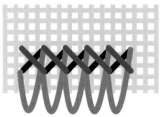

Repeat from step 1. For a fringed edge, cut loops to an even length.

Long-legged Cross Stitch

Worked in a single line, this gives a braided effect.

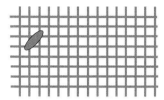

Start by making a diagonal stitch to the right over two horizontal and two vertical threads.

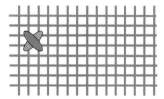

Complete a single cross stitch by making a diagonal stitch to the left over the first stitch, (darker colour).

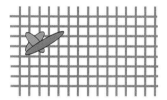

Start the long-legged bit by working a diagonal stitch to the right, to cover the existing stitches, over two horizontal threads and four vertical threads, (darker colour).

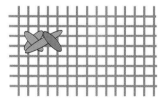

Take a diagonal stitch back over the long stitch, crossing two horizontal threads and two vertical threads, (darker colour).

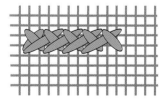

Continue to work over four threads to the right and back over two threads to the left.

NEEDLEWORK

For needlework enthusiasts I include some cushions and rugs. If you are used to working with charts and cross stitch or tent stitch (petite point) for making miniature carpets, etc. there is little explanation necessary. For those who are not, I would suggest that you consult one of the many books which explain the techniques in detail, this is beyond the scope of the present book.

All the designs were worked using DMC stranded embroidery thread and have the DMC numbers as a guide. A fine crewel wool could be used for rugs, such as Appletons Crewel Wool. There are hundreds of shades to choose from and this would give a more matte finish to the work.

These cushions can be worked on fine canvas or evenweave fabric of 18, 22, 24 or 32 count. Some designs use the usual traditional tapestry stitch – tent stitch, some just use long stitch, with the stitching arranged to cover all the canvas.

A magnifying glass of some kind is very useful to be able to see your stitching more easily. I use one that is suspended from a cord around the neck. They are readily available from needlework shops, or by mail order.

EMBROIDERED CUSHIONS

Although these cushions are very small, they can easily be worked with very simple basic embroidery stitches, using just one strand of embroidery thread. Cut a usable length of stranded embroidery cotton and separate one strand from the six. You will need a rectangle of fine fabric cut larger than you will eventually use. This makes it easier to handle during the embroidery process. The stitches I used were lazy daisy stitch, French knot, bullion stitch and stem stitch.

Stitched Cushions & Rugs

BIRD CUSHION

This cushion is best worked in tent stitch or half cross stitch on very fine even weave fabric, but it can also be worked in cross stitch if you prefer. Using 28 count fabric the finished size is 1½ x 1½in (39 x 39mm), on 32 count fabric 1¼ x 1¼in (34 x 34mm).

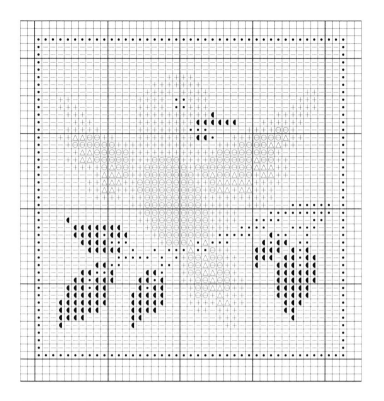

Colour key: Bird cushion

—	= DMC : Blanc
△	= DMC : 726
◖	= DMC : 833
●	= DMC : 680
⊖	= DMC : 813
+	= DMC : 826

BARGELLO STITCH MINIATURE CUSHIONS AND RUGS

As a complete change from the usual cross stitch or tent stitch miniature embroidery, a quick and easy alternative is Bargello stitch. I always think that it is somewhat of a misnomer to call this Bargello stitch, because it is really a series of straight stitches, worked over varying numbers of threads. Using fine count canvas with a suitable number of strands of embroidery thread, usually two or perhaps three, it really covers the canvas quickly. Just keep stitching, taking the thread over and over so that there is a good padding on the back of the work, changing colours as necessary.

BARGELLO CUSHIONS

Five cushions in Bargello stitch. Use these as working charts. Working in a similar way, it is relatively easy to produce interesting patterns. Some of these are shown in the photograph (p. 151).

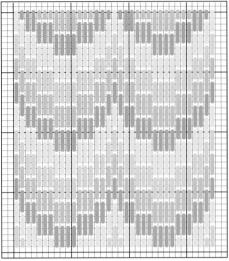

Miniature Bargello stitch cushion Pattern 3

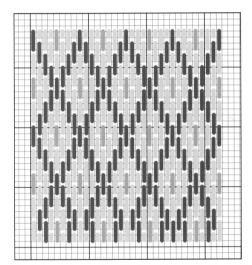

Miniature Bargello stitch cushion Pattern 1

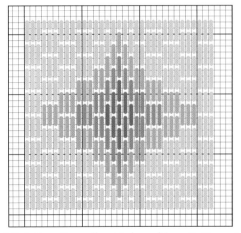

Miniature Bargello stitch cushion Pattern 4

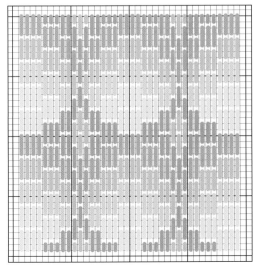

Miniature Bargello stitch cushion Pattern 5

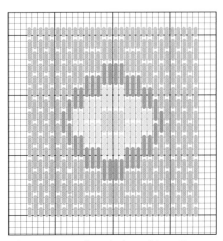

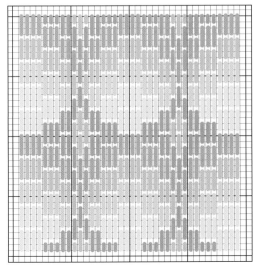

Miniature Bargello stitch cushion Pattern 2

Miniature Bargello stitch cushion Pattern 5

BARGELLO RUG

Bargello rug, which serves as a working chart. The colour choice is up to you.
The other patterns used for the cushions can be modified in a similar way.

PORTUGUESE STYLE RUGS AND MATCHING CUSHIONS

For those who enjoy working in cross stitch, here are a few examples based on actual Portuguese designs. The originals would be worked in what the Portuguese know as Pont d'Arriolos stitch on a heavy Hessian material. This is a variation of what is known in England as long-legged cross stitch. They are still made today, although because of the time involved in hand stitching, the genuine ones are very expensive. Making rugs and cushions at home is becoming an increasingly popular pastime. Therefore, miniature rugs worked in cross stitch are most appropriate.

My versions are worked in DMC stranded embroidery cotton on fine canvas. The count of the canvas obviously makes a difference to the finished sizes of the articles. The cushions were worked using 22 or 24 count canvas, and the rugs on 18 count canvas. These are intended to be worked in cross stitch.

Charts for working the designs are included showing both a colour cross stitch version and a more easily followed black and white chart using symbols, together with a key to the DMC threads used for the originals.

Many of the Portuguese traditional designs have each motif outlined with a single row of stitches, which is in fact the first bit to be stitched when making a full size rug. The filling of the motifs comes next and lastly the background. In miniature this is not practicable. To attain a slightly more authentic look, rug 3 is virtually rug 2 with back stitching outlines and an additional border. The back stitching looks best worked with a couple of strands of embroidery thread, and worked individually for each square, not taken in long stitches.

CUSHIONS

These are designed to match the rugs which come later, and should be worked in cross stitch on fine count canvas or fabric. They are shown below in coloured cross stitch, with black and white working charts. You can, of course, change the colours to match in with your decor.

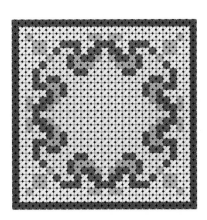

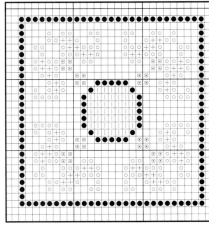
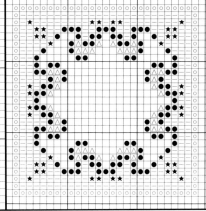
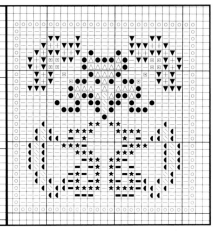

Colour key

—	= DMC : Ecru	+	= DMC : 761
◣	= DMC : 824	▼	= DMC : 3328
★	= DMC : 783	⊡	= DMC : 503
╲	= DMC : 840	△	= DMC : 809
▬	= DMC : 680	●	= DMC : 826
	= DMC : 948		

Backstitch key

———	= DMC : 824
———	= DMC : 840
┄┄┄	= DMC : 221
———	= DMC : 3363

Key to working charts for Portuguese cushions and rugs

RUGS

Portuguese style rugs, shown in coloured cross stitch, with the working charts. Colour codes for the threads I used are shown on the previous page. You can change these to your own choice of colours of course. Appleton crewel wool is a good alternative thread, giving a matte finish. This was used for the rug shown on page 160.

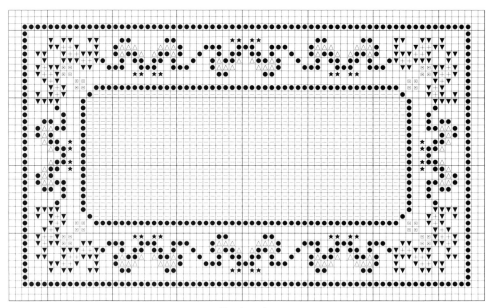

Design 1

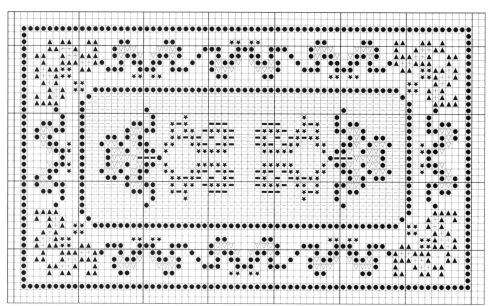

Design 2

Design 3

Pattern 1

Pattern 2

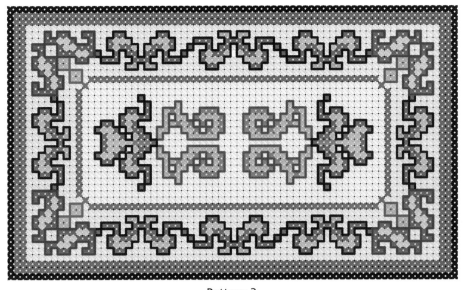

Pattern 3

Portuguese rug, pattern 1, stitched using alternative 'tent stitch' and Appleton crewel wool. For the fringe, see p. 152.

Conversion Tables

Fractions of an Inch

In ¹⁄₃₂ in increments, with metric equivalents correct to one decimal place.

in	mm	in	mm	in	mm	in	mm
¹⁄₃₂	0.8	⁹⁄₃₂	7.1	¹⁷⁄₃₂	13.5	²⁵⁄₃₂	19.8
¹⁄₁₆	1.6	⁵⁄₁₆	7.9	⁹⁄₁₆	14.3	¹³⁄₁₆	20.6
³⁄₃₂	2.4	¹¹⁄₃₂	8.7	¹⁹⁄₃₂	15.1	²⁷⁄₃₂	21.4
⅛	3.2	⅜	9.5	⅝	15.9	⅞	22.2
⁵⁄₃₂	4.0	¹³⁄₃₂	10.3	²¹⁄₃₂	16.7	²⁹⁄₃₂	23.0
³⁄₁₆	4.8	⁷⁄₁₆	11.1	¹¹⁄₁₆	17.5	¹⁵⁄₁₆	23.8
⁷⁄₃₂	5.6	¹⁵⁄₃₂	11.9	²³⁄₃₂	18	³¹⁄₃₂	24.6
¼	6.4	½	12.7	¾	19.1	1	25.4

Inches plus Fractions

Metric equivalents are corrected to one decimal place

in	0	1	2	3	4	5	6	7	8	9	10
0		25.4	50.8	76.2	101.6	127.0	152.4	177.8	203.2	228.6	254.0
¹⁄₁₆	1.6	27.0	52.4	77.8	103.2	128.6	154.0	179.4	204.8	230.2	255.6
⅛	3.2	28.6	54.0	79.4	104.8	130.2	155.6	181.0	206.4	231.8	257.2
³⁄₁₆	4.8	30.2	55.6	81.0	106.4	131.8	157.2	182.6	208.0	233.4	258.8
¼	6.4	31.8	57.2	82.6	108.0	133.4	158.8	184.2	209.6	235.0	260.4
⁵⁄₁₆	7.9	33.3	58.7	84.1	109.5	134.9	160.3	185.7	211.1	236.5	261.9
⅜	9.5	34.9	60.3	85.7	111.1	136.5	161.9	187.3	212.7	238.1	263.5
⁷⁄₁₆	11.1	36.5	61.9	87.3	112.7	138.1	163.5	188.9	214.3	239.7	265.1
½	12.7	38.1	63.5	88.9	114.3	139.7	165.1	190.5	215.9	241.3	266.7
⁹⁄₁₆	14.3	39.7	65.1	90.5	115.9	141.3	166.7	192.1	217.5	242.9	268.3
⅝	15.9	41.3	66.7	92.1	117.5	142.9	168.3	193.7	219.1	244.5	269.9
¹¹⁄₁₆	17.5	42.9	68.3	93.7	119.1	144.5	169.9	195.3	220.7	246.1	271.5
¾	19.1	44.5	69.9	95.3	120.7	146.1	171.5	196.9	222.3	247.7	273.1
¹³⁄₁₆	20.6	46.0	71.4	96.8	122.2	147.6	173.0	198.4	223.8	249.2	274.6
⅞	22.2	47.6	73.0	98.4	123.8	149.2	174.6	200.0	225.4	250.8	276.2
¹⁵⁄₁₆	23.8	49.2	74.6	100.0	125.4	150.8	176.2	201.6	227.0	252.4	277.8

Acknowledgements

I would like to thank the following companies for their support and assistance:

Axminster Power Tool Centre
Chard Street, Axminster, Devon, EX13 5DZ
Tel 0800 371822/01297 35242
email: mail@axminster.co.uk
www.axminster.co.uk

Blackwells of Hawkwell
The Old Maltings, 5 Weir Pond Road, Rochford, Essex SS4 1AH
Tel 01702 544211
email: sales@blackwells-miniatures.co.uk
www.blackwells-miniatures.co.uk

Fred Aldous
37 Lever Street, Manchester MI 1LW
Tel 0161 236 4224
email: aldous@btinternet.com
www.fredaldous.co.ukW.HobbyLtd

Sew Simple
Unit 16, Taverham Craft Centre, Fir Covert Road, Taverham, Norwich, NR8 6HT
Tel 01603 262870
www.sew-simple.co.uk

W. Hobby Ltd
Knight's Hill Square, London SE27 0HH
Tel 020 8761 4244
email: mail@hobby.uk.com
http://www.hobby.uk.com

I would also like to express my grateful thanks to David Arscott, my editor, for his patience and good humour in the face of the adversities which have befallen us during the production of this book.

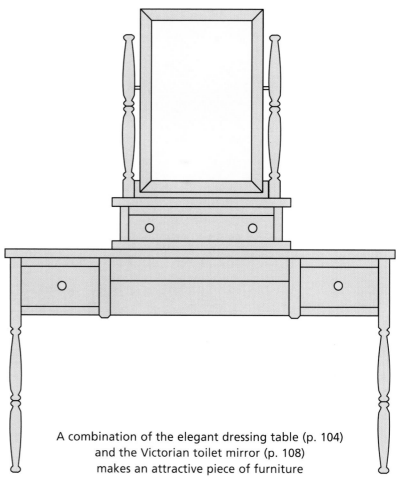

A combination of the elegant dressing table (p. 104) and the Victorian toilet mirror (p. 108) makes an attractive piece of furniture

Index

Page numbers in **bold** refer to projects with templates

GMC Publications

BOOKS

WOODCARVING

Beginning Woodcarving	GMC Publications
Carving Architectural Detail in Wood: The Classical Tradition	
	Frederick Wilbur
Carving Birds & Beasts	GMC Publications
Carving Classical Styles in Wood	Frederick Wilbur
Carving the Human Figure: Studies in Wood and Stone	Dick Onians
Carving Nature: Wildlife Studies in Wood	Frank Fox-Wilson
Celtic Carved Lovespoons: 30 Patterns	Sharon Littley & Clive Griffin
Decorative Woodcarving (New Edition)	Jeremy Williams
Elements of Woodcarving	Chris Pye
Figure Carving in Wood: Human and Animal Forms	Sara Wilkinson
Lettercarving in Wood: A Practical Course	Chris Pye
Relief Carving in Wood: A Practical Introduction	Chris Pye
Woodcarving for Beginners	GMC Publications
Woodcarving Made Easy	Cynthia Rogers
Woodcarving Tools, Materials & Equipment (New Edition in 2 vols.)	
	Chris Pye

WOODTURNING

Bowl Turning Techniques Masterclass	Tony Boase
Chris Child's Projects for Woodturners	Chris Child
Decorating Turned Wood: The Maker's Eye	Liz & Michael O'Donnell
Green Woodwork	Mike Abbott
A Guide to Work-Holding on the Lathe	Fred Holder
Keith Rowley's Woodturning Projects	Keith Rowley
Making Screw Threads in Wood	Fred Holder
Segmented Turning: A Complete Guide	Ron Hampton
Turned Boxes: 50 Designs	Chris Stott
Turning Green Wood	Michael O'Donnell
Turning Pens and Pencils	Kip Christensen & Rex Burningham
Wood for Woodturners	Mark Baker
Woodturning: Forms and Materials	John Hunnex
Woodturning: A Foundation Course (New Edition)	Keith Rowley
Woodturning: A Fresh Approach	Robert Chapman
Woodturning: An Individual Approach	Dave Regester
Woodturning: A Source Book of Shapes	John Hunnex
Woodturning Masterclass	Tony Boase
Woodturning Projects: A Workshop Guide to Shapes	Mark Baker

WOODWORKING

Beginning Picture Marquetry	Lawrence Threadgold
Carcass Furniture	GMC Publications
Celtic Carved Lovespoons: 30 Patterns	Sharon Littley & Clive Griffin
Celtic Woodcraft	Glenda Bennett
Celtic Woodworking Projects	Glenda Bennett
Complete Woodfinishing (Revised Edition)	Ian Hosker
David Charlesworth's Furniture-Making Techniques	
	David Charlesworth
David Charlesworth's Furniture-Making Techniques – Volume 2	
	David Charlesworth
Furniture Projects with the Router	Kevin Ley
Furniture Restoration (Practical Crafts)	Kevin Jan Bonner
Furniture Restoration: A Professional at Work	John Lloyd

Furniture Workshop	Kevin Ley
Green Woodwork	Mike Abbott
History of Furniture: Ancient to 1900	Michael Huntley
Intarsia: 30 Patterns for the Scrollsaw	John Everett
Making Heirloom Boxes	Peter Lloyd
Making Screw Threads in Wood	Fred Holder
Making Woodwork Aids and Devices	Robert Wearing
Mastering the Router	Ron Fox
Pine Furniture Projects for the Home	Dave Mackenzie
Router Magic: Jigs, Fixtures and Tricks to Unleash your Router's Full Potential	Bill Hylton
Router Projects for the Home	GMC Publications
Router Tips & Techniques	Robert Wearing
Routing: A Workshop Handbook	Anthony Bailey
Routing for Beginners (Revised and Expanded Edition)	Anthony Bailey
Stickmaking: A Complete Course	Andrew Jones & Clive George
Stickmaking Handbook	Andrew Jones & Clive George
Storage Projects for the Router	GMC Publications
Success with Sharpening	Ralph Laughton
Veneering: A Complete Course	Ian Hosker
Veneering Handbook	Ian Hosker
Wood: Identification & Use	Terry Porter
Woodworking Techniques and Projects	Anthony Bailey
Woodworking with the Router: Professional Router Techniques any Woodworker can Use	
	Bill Hylton & Fred Matlack

UPHOLSTERY

Upholstery: A Beginners' Guide	David James
Upholstery: A Complete Course (Revised Edition)	David James
Upholstery Restoration	David James
Upholstery Techniques & Projects	David James
Upholstery Tips and Hints	David James

DOLLS' HOUSES AND MINIATURES

1/12 Scale Character Figures for the Dolls' House	James Carrington
Americana in 1/12 Scale: 50 Authentic Projects	
	Joanne Ogreenc & Mary Lou Santovec
The Authentic Georgian Dolls' House	Brian Long
A Beginners' Guide to the Dolls' House Hobby	Jean Nisbett
Celtic, Medieval and Tudor Wall Hangings in 1/12 Scale Needlepoint	
	Sandra Whitehead
Creating Decorative Fabrics: Projects in 1/12 Scale	Janet Storey
Dolls' House Accessories, Fixtures and Fittings	Andrea Barham
Dolls' House Furniture: Easy-to-Make Projects in 1/12 Scale	Freida Gray
Dolls' House Makeovers	Jean Nisbett
Dolls' House Window Treatments	Eve Harwood
Edwardian-Style Hand-Knitted Fashion for 1/12 Scale Dolls	
	Yvonne Wakefield
How to Make Your Dolls' House Special: Fresh Ideas for Decorating	
	Beryl Armstrong
Making 1/12 Scale Wicker Furniture for the Dolls' House	Sheila Smith

CRAFTS

GARDENING

MAGAZINES

Woodturning ◆ Woodcarving ◆ Furniture & Cabinetmaking
The Router ◆ New Woodworking ◆ The Dolls' House Magazine
Outdoor Photography ◆ Black & White Photography
Knitting ◆ Guild News

The above represents a full list of all titles currently published or scheduled to be published.
All are available direct from the Publishers or through bookshops, newsagents and specialist retailers.
To place an order, or to obtain a complete catalogue, contact:

GMC Publications,
Castle Place, 166 High Street, Lewes, East Sussex BN7 1XU United Kingdom
Tel: 01273 488005 Fax: 01273 402866
E-mail: pubs@thegmcgroup.com
Website: www.gmcbooks.com

Orders by credit card are accepted